VILLAGE SCHOOL

photographs by Bryn Campbell

For Tom,
Bryn Campbell

COMUS BOOKS

For the children, their parents and staff, of Elsted District Village School. And, above all, for the Headmistress, my wife Audrey, who made both the project and the book possible.

FOREWORD

These photographs of Elsted District Primary School, Sussex, were taken from 1972-73. It was not an assignment but a labour of love.

Throughout my career, I have set myself a succession of long-term projects outside the constraints and compromises of professional work.

This particular subject attracted me for many reasons, all rather confused now in my memory. But it was largely as a reaction against years of involvement, both as picture editor and photographer, in reporting violence, misery and high-profile events. I wanted to reaffirm, if only to myself, the importance and satisfaction of photographing more normal, everyday life.

Lewis Hine once said, "There were two things I wanted to do. I wanted to show the things that had to be corrected. I wanted to show the things that had to be appreciated." It was time, I felt, to concentrate on the latter.

Photographing Elsted School in detail seemed an appealing, worthwhile and practical proposition. It was near my home, my wife was the Headmistress, giving me an obvious advantage, and my expenses would be limited to the cost of materials.

Knowing my usual reluctance to end a project, I set a time-limit of just one school year. After obtaining official permission, I visited the school for two or three days almost every week. The children soon took my presence for granted and then I was able to photograph freely and unobtrusively.

Elsted was a small, rural village school with some 30 infant and junior pupils, the teaching Head, one full-time and one part-time teacher, a welfare assistant, and two cooks to prepare the midday meal. Parents helped out in all manner of ways and there were close links with the local church.

It may sound a cliche but life at the school was genuinely like being part of a large, happy family. I covered as many activities as possible, though it was never my intention to produce a comprehensive record. My interests were more aesthetic than documentary. Similarly, in editing the pictures for this book, I simply selected my favourite images.

At the end of the year, a large selection of prints was exhibited at the school itself, and later, nearby, at the Chichester 900 Festival.

Sadly, Elsted School no longer exists. The dwindling number of pupils made it uneconomic to maintain. I hope this book gives some flavour of how special it once was.

BRYN CAMPBELL

1

2

3

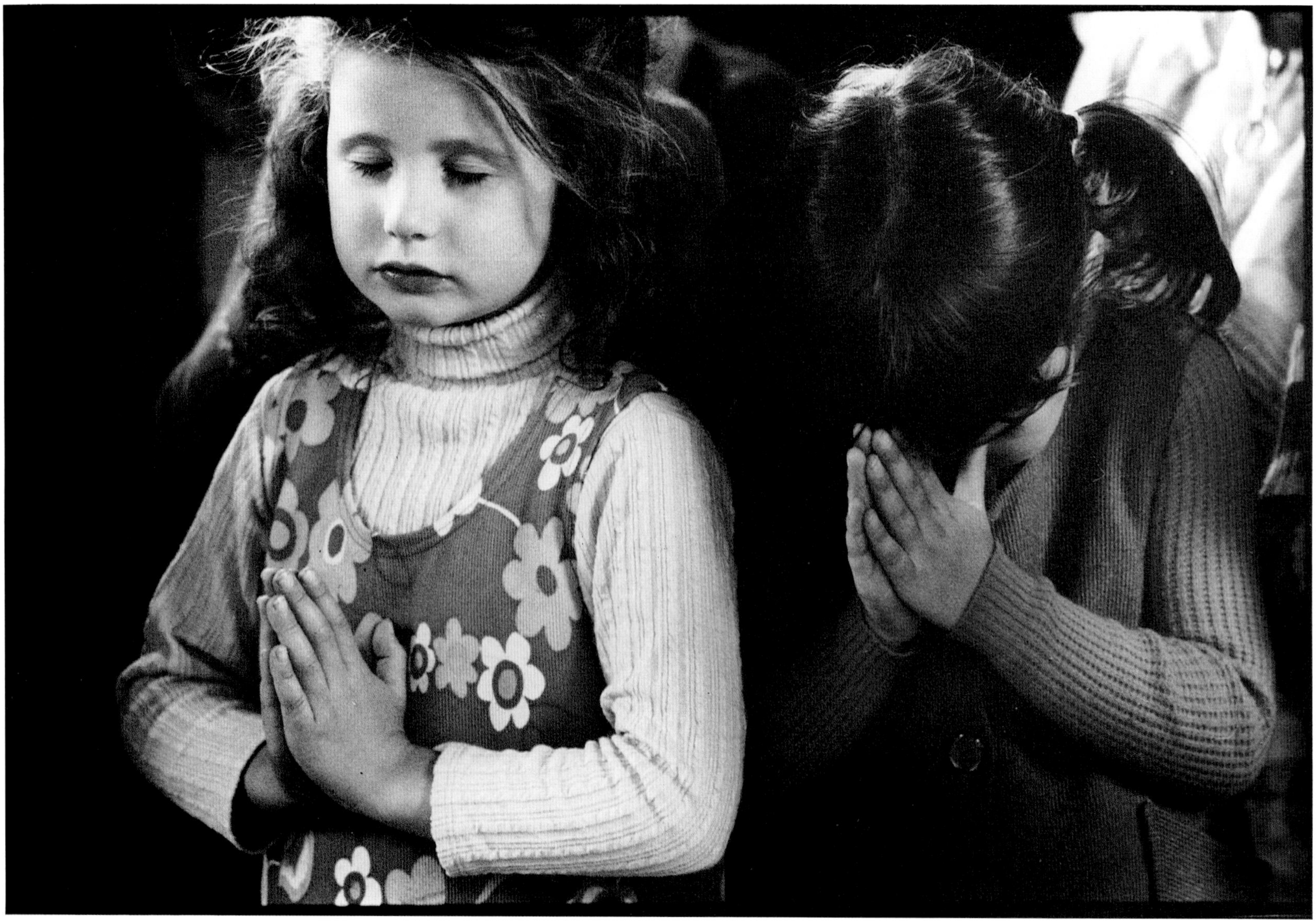

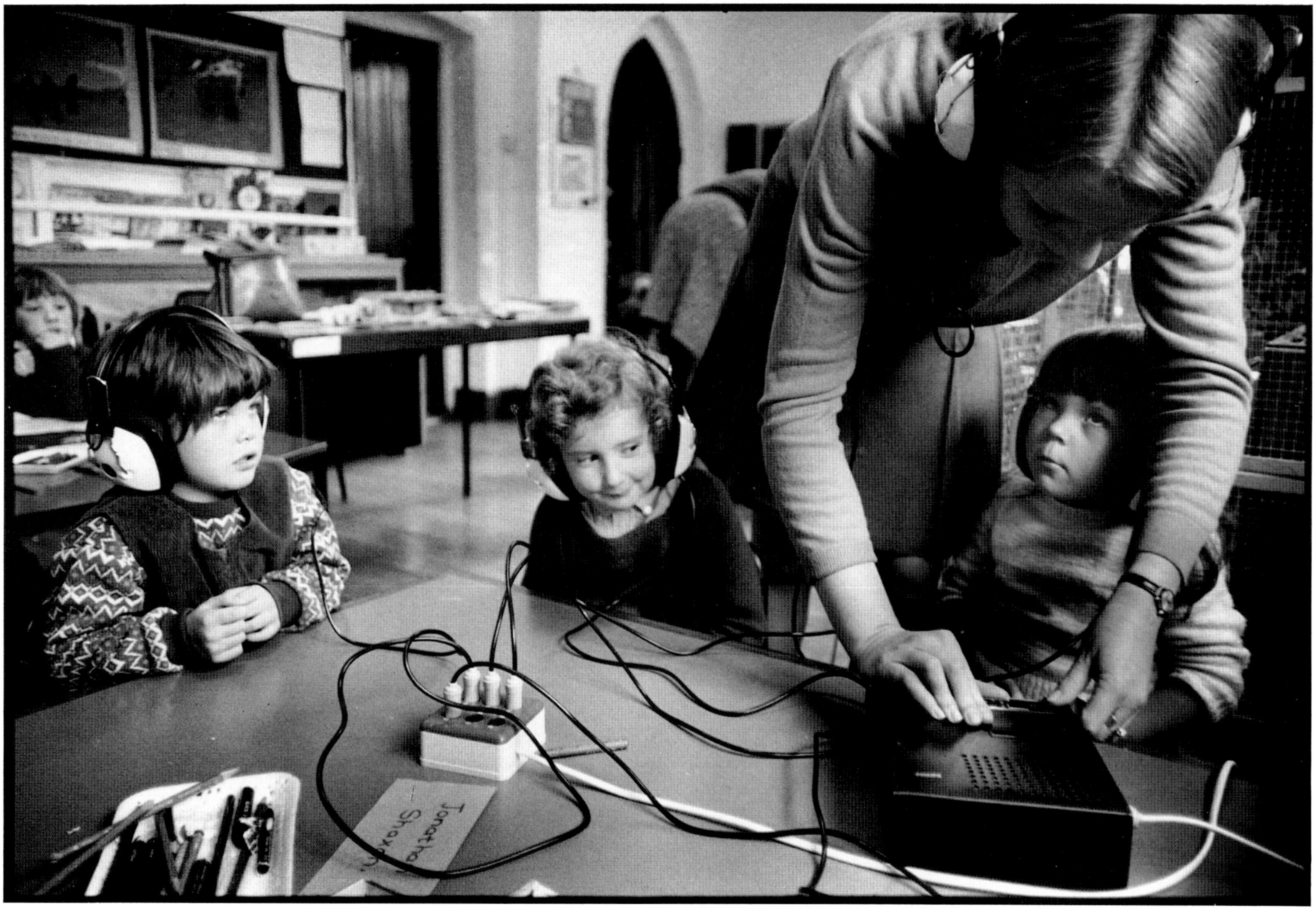

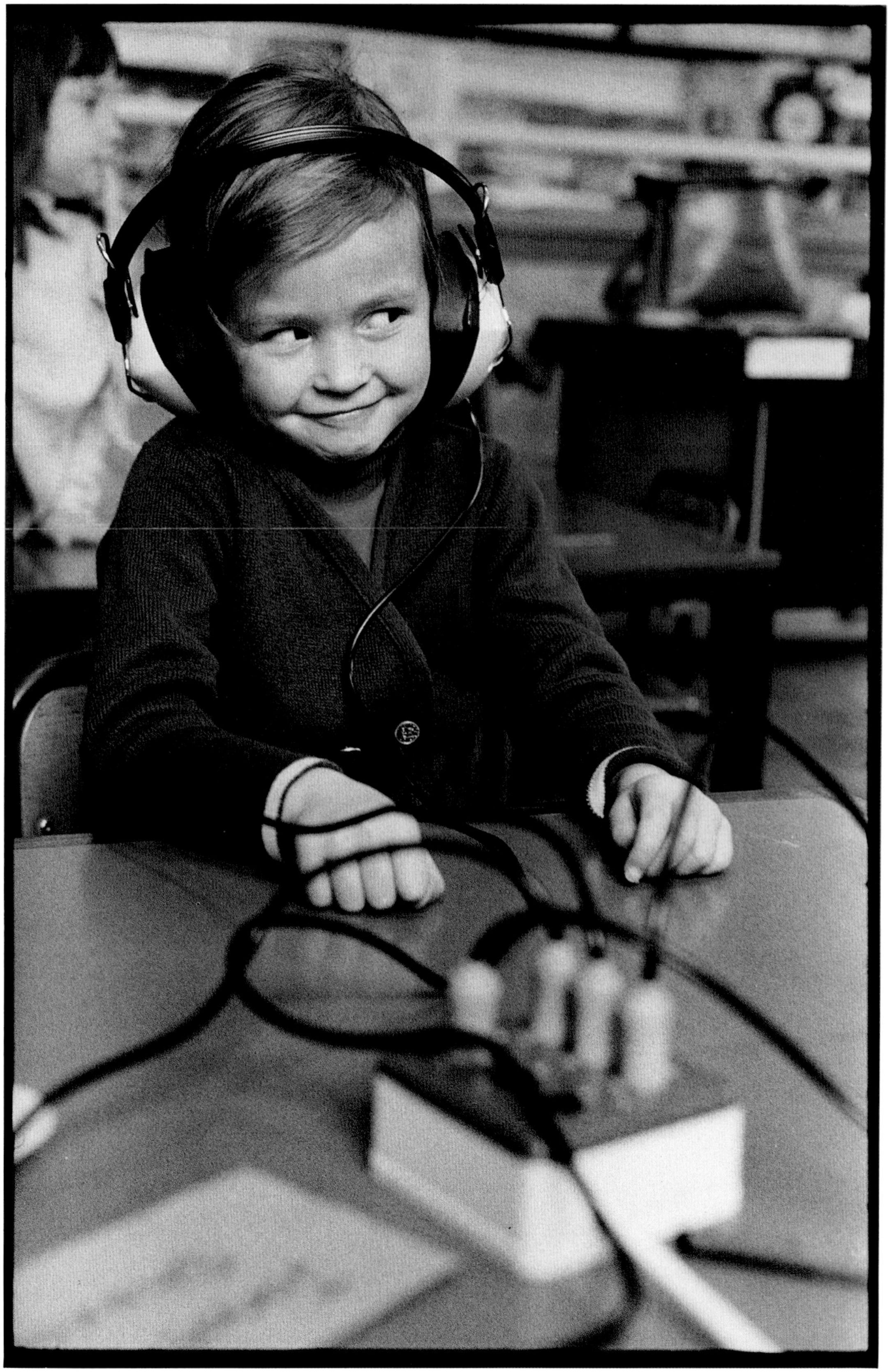

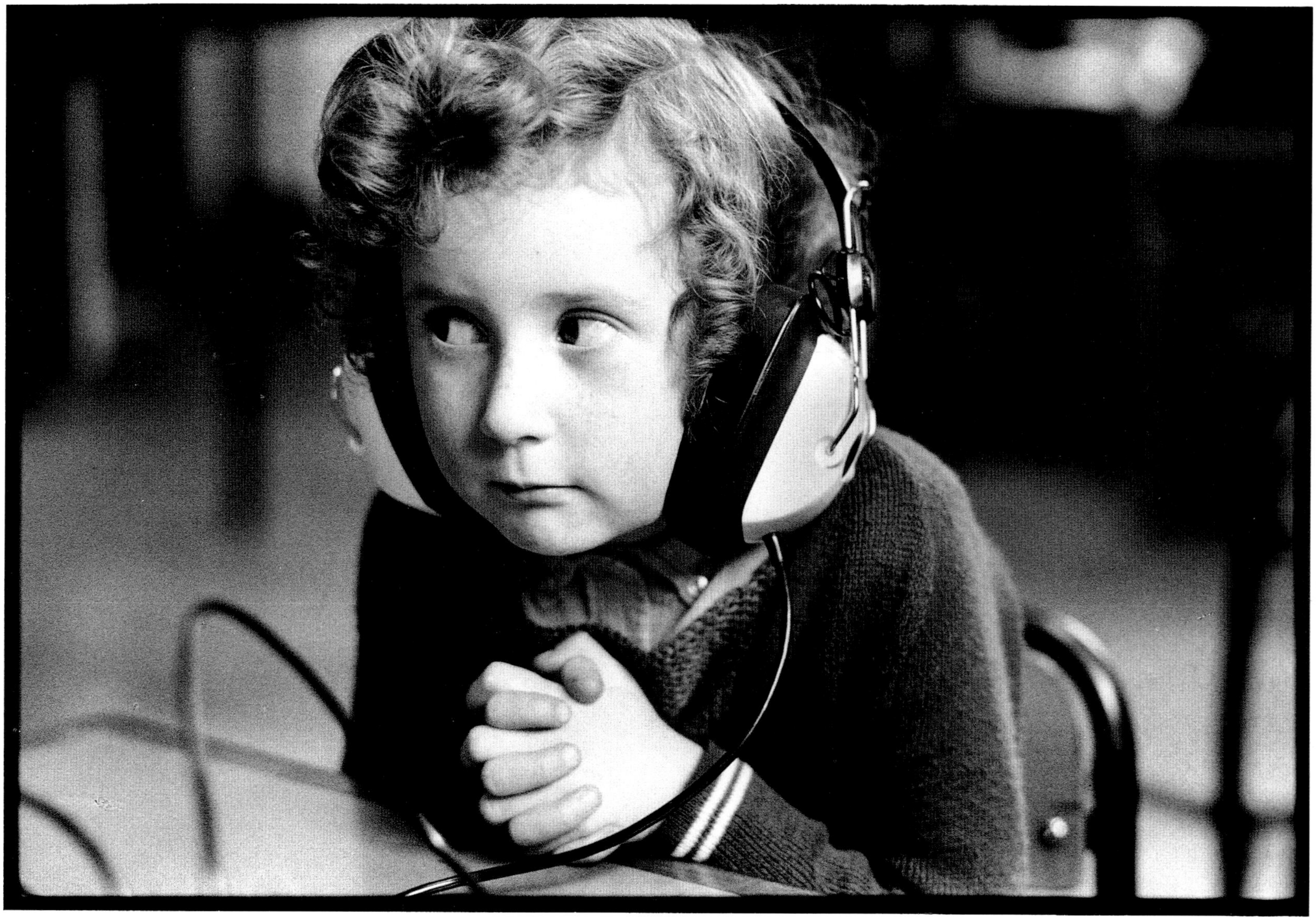

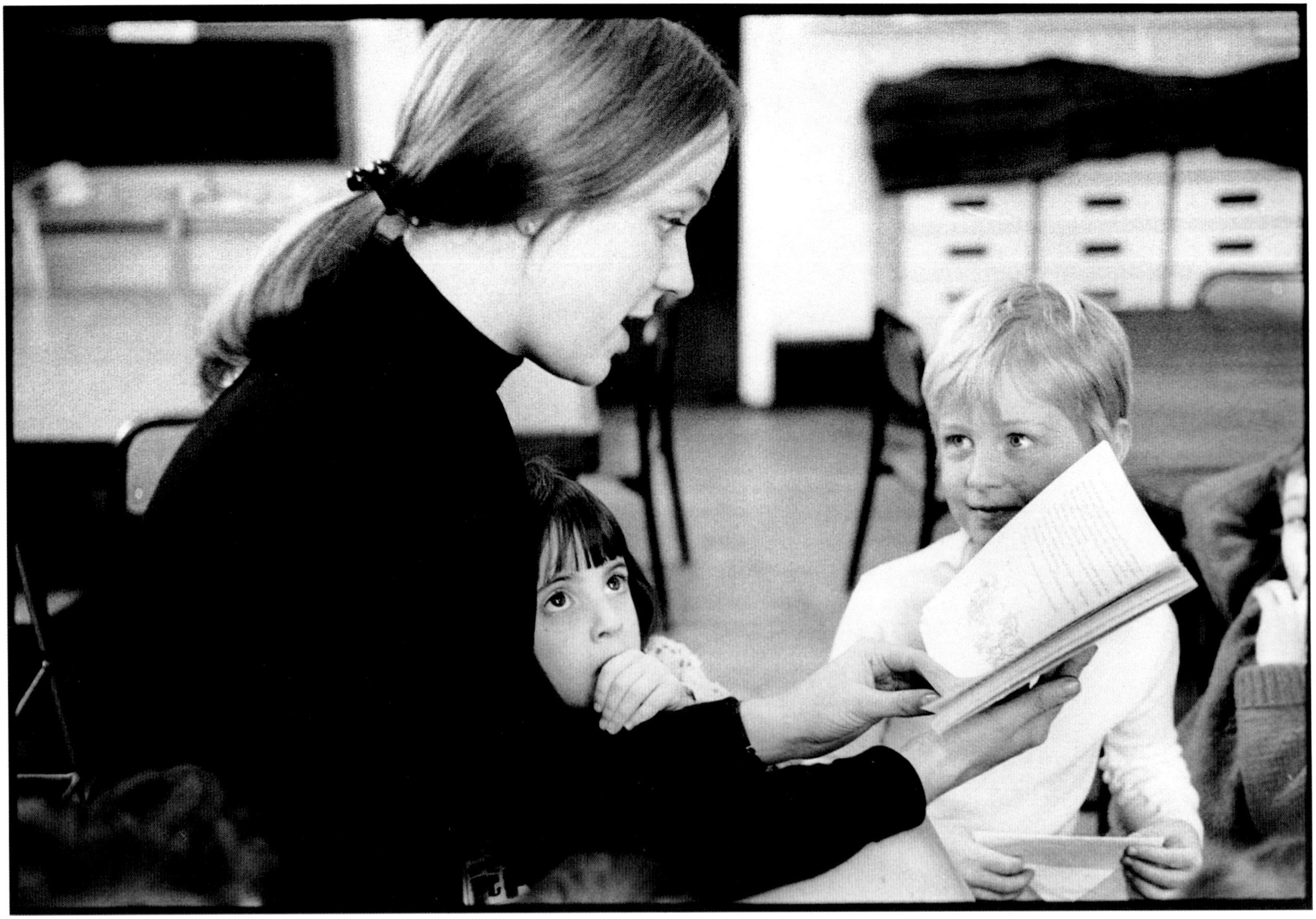

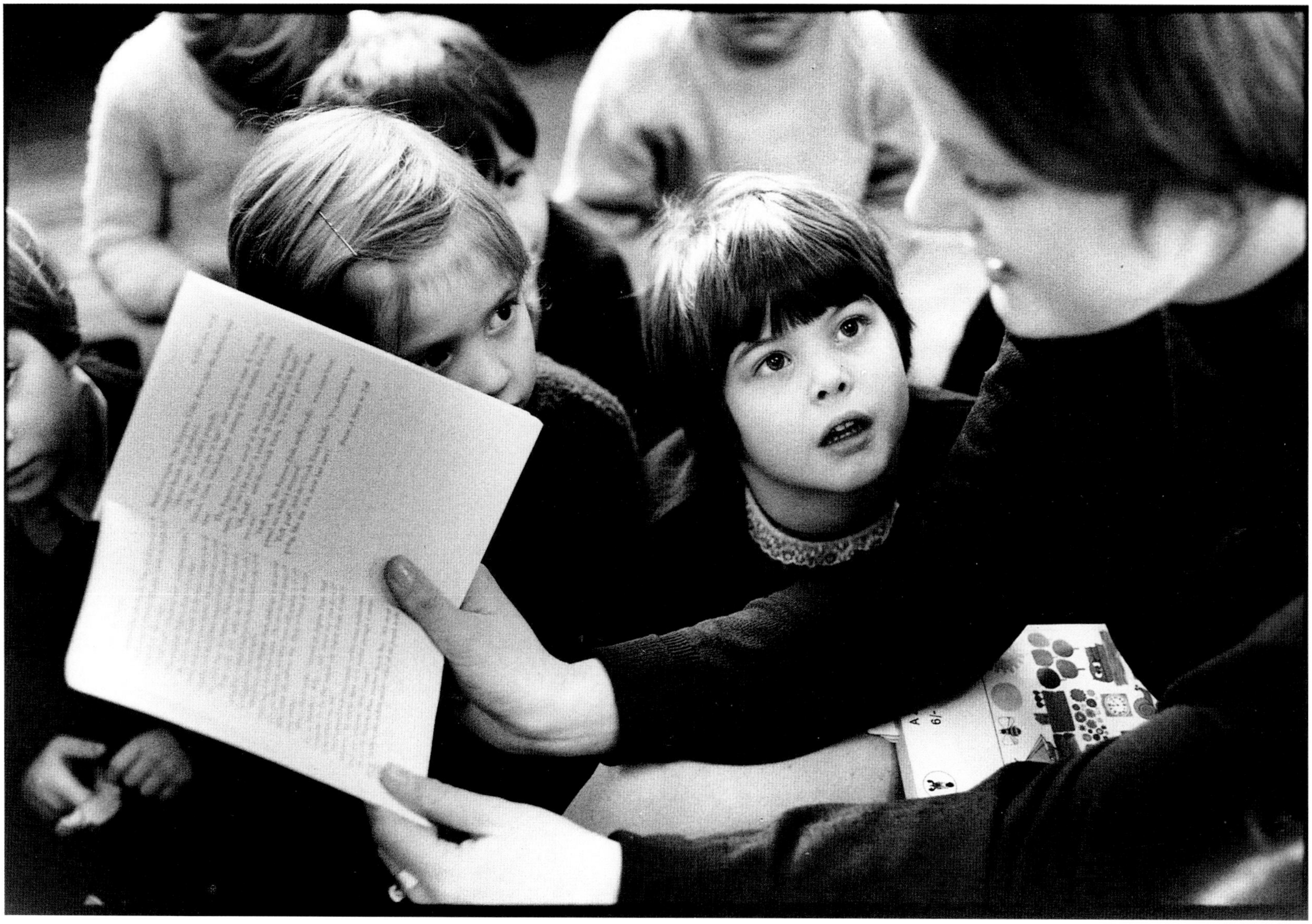

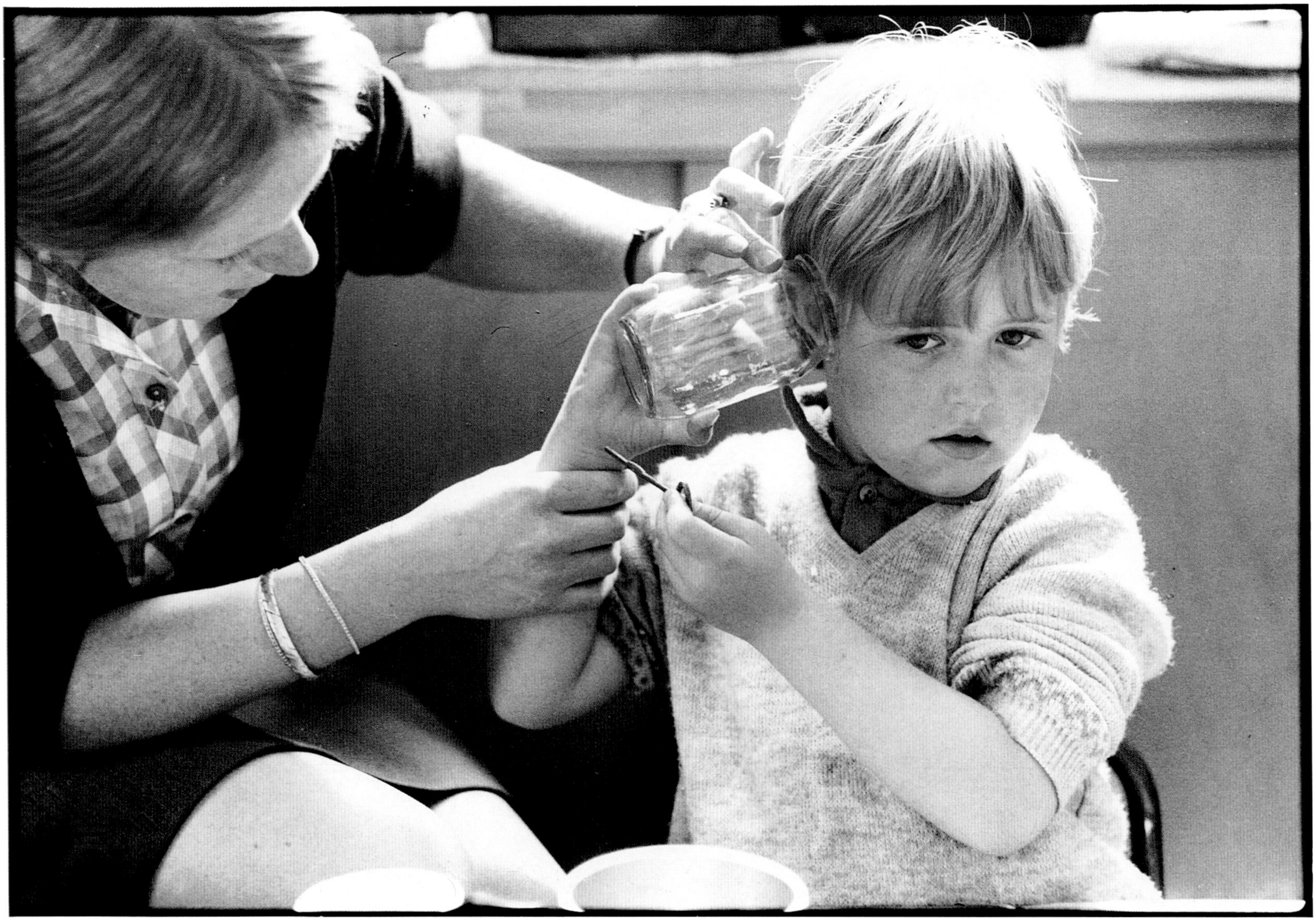

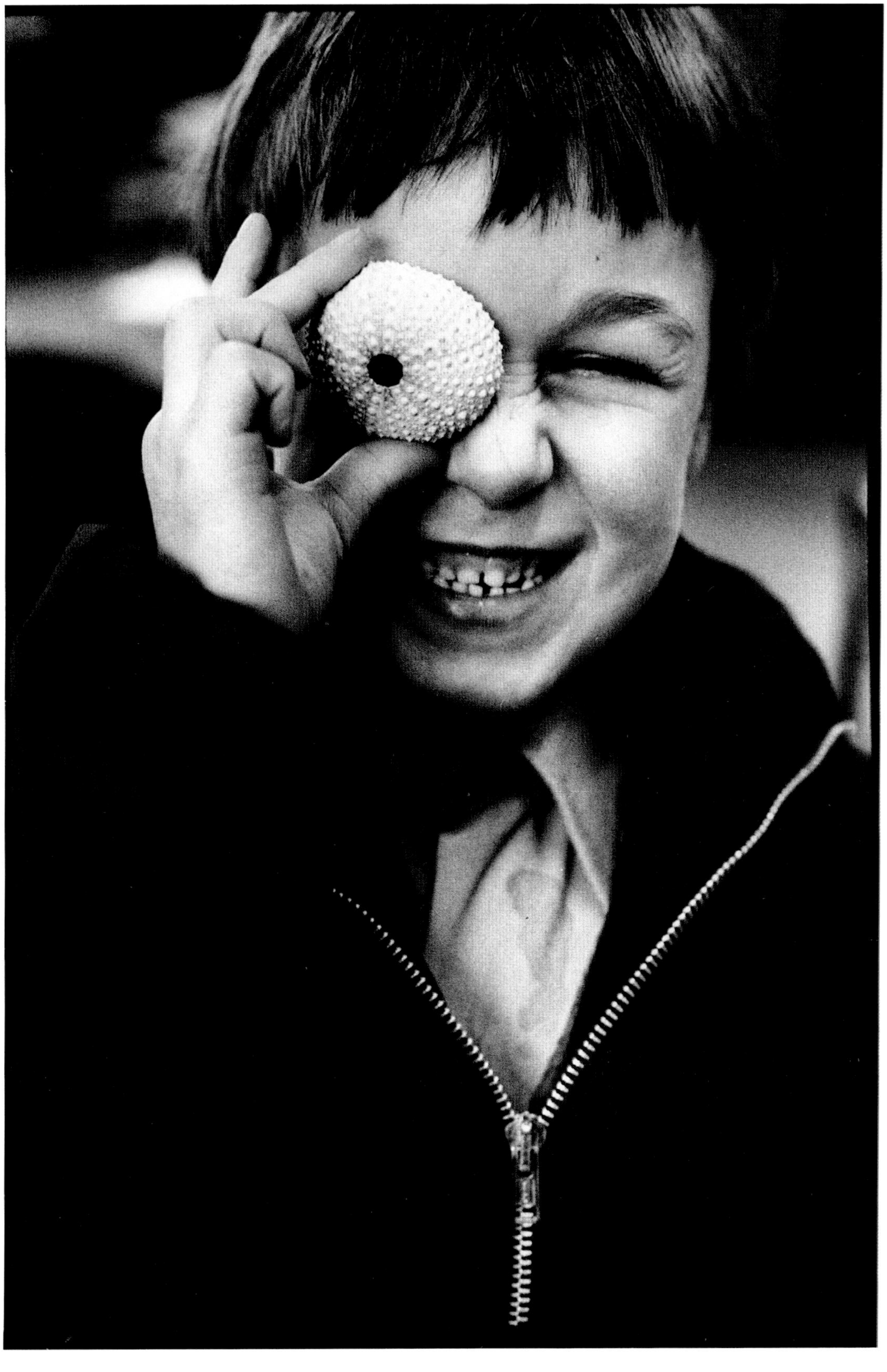

12

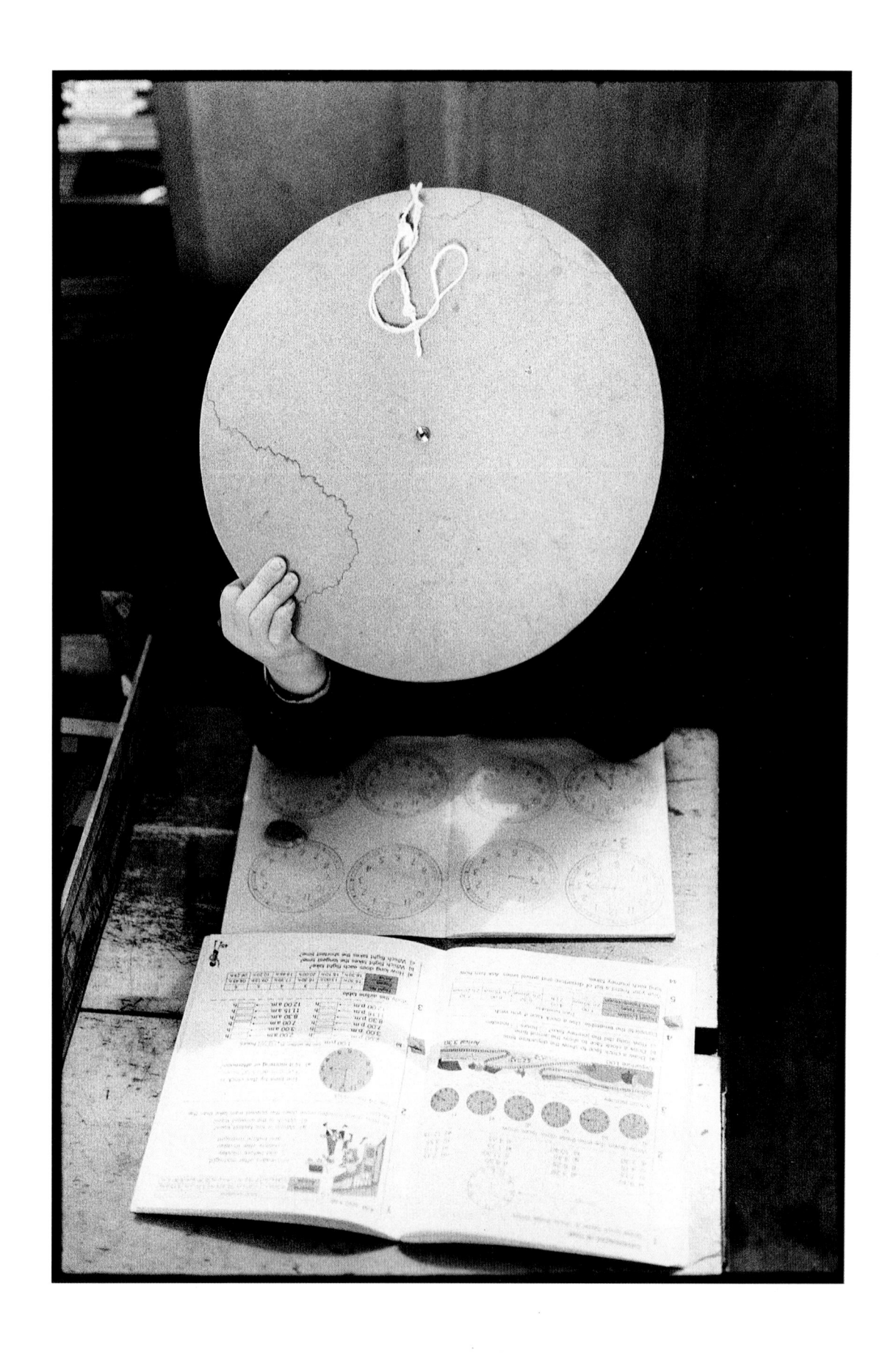

13

14

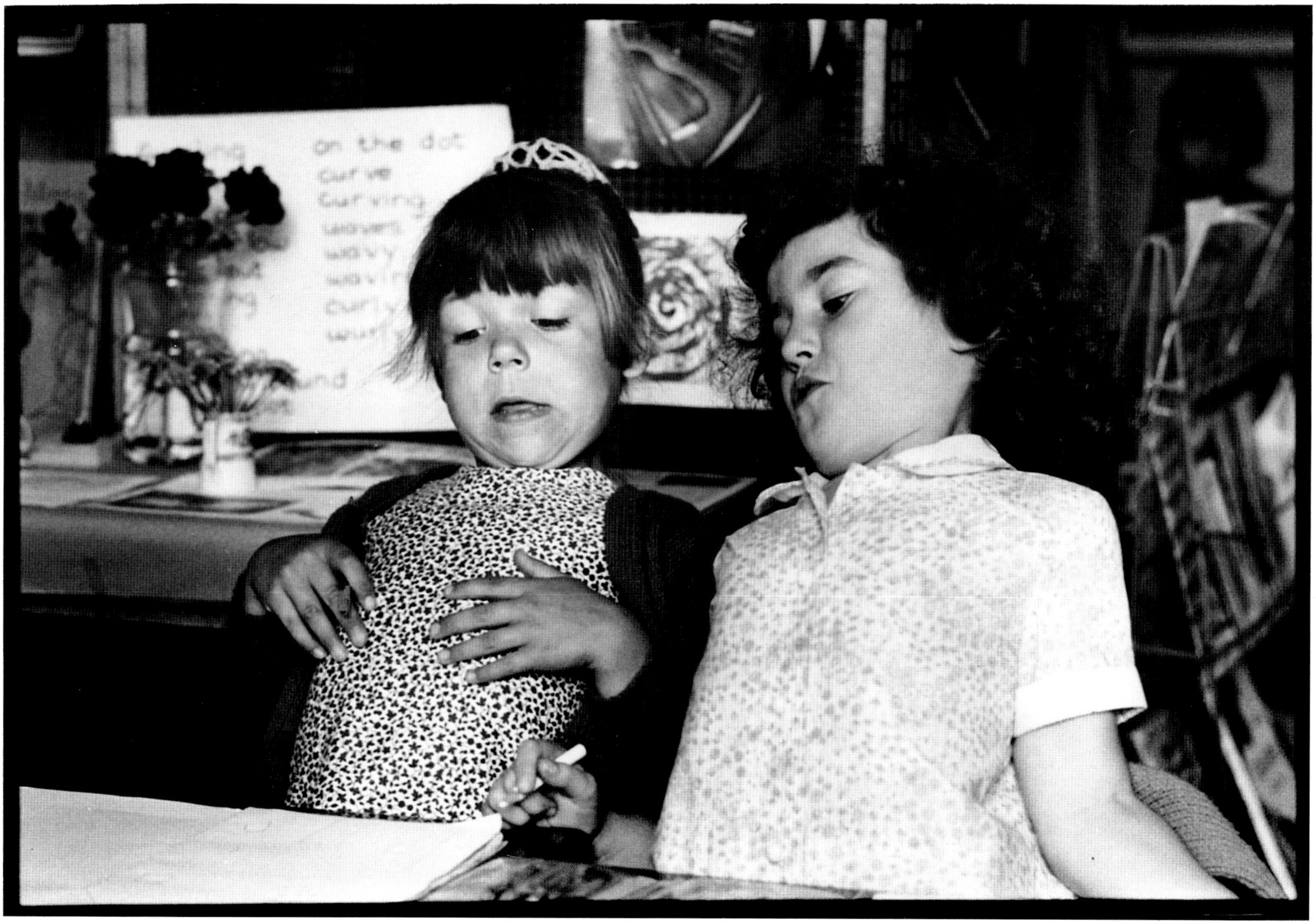
on the dot
curve
curving
waves
wavy

16

17

18

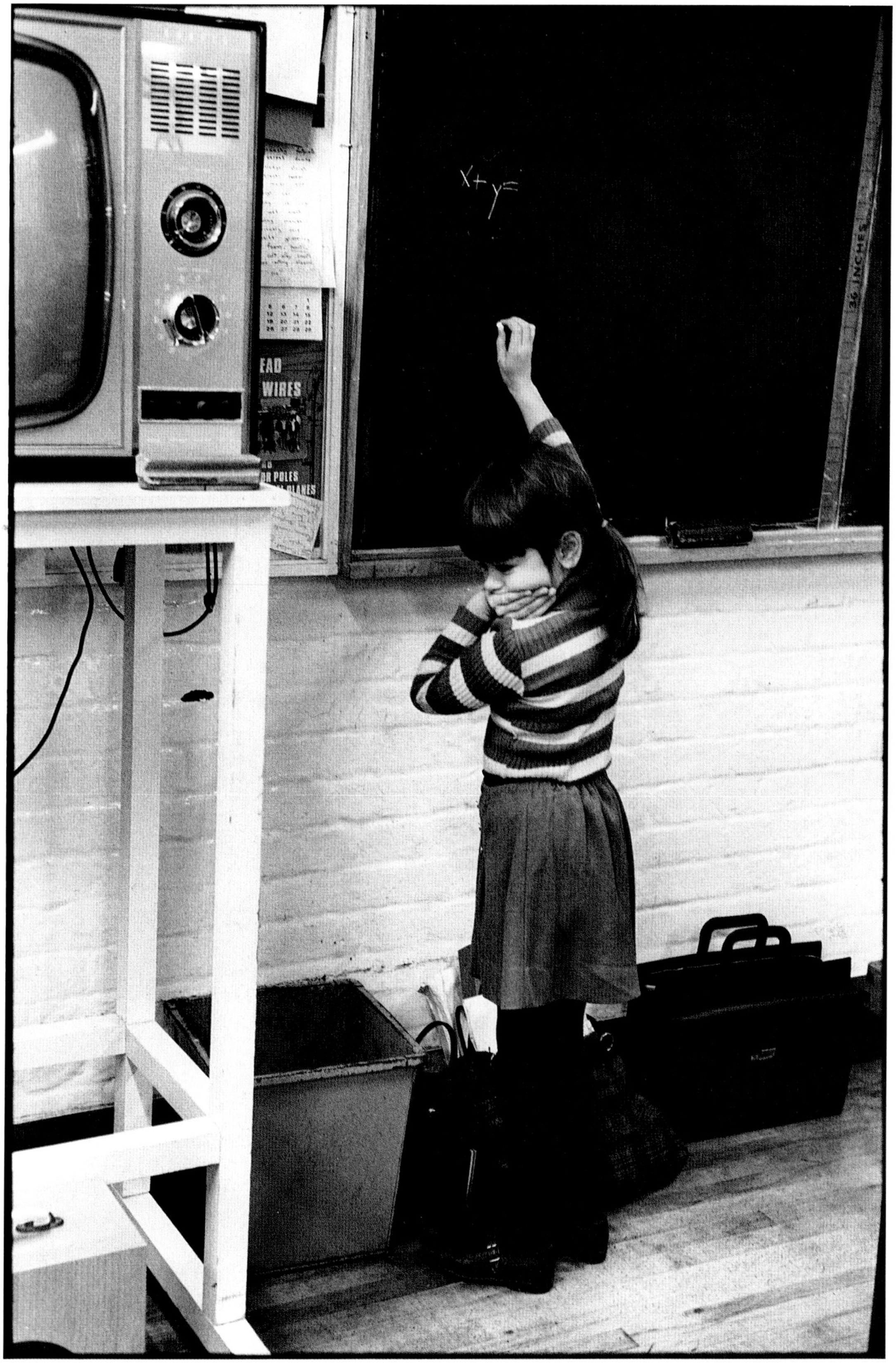
x+y=
36 INCHES
WIRES

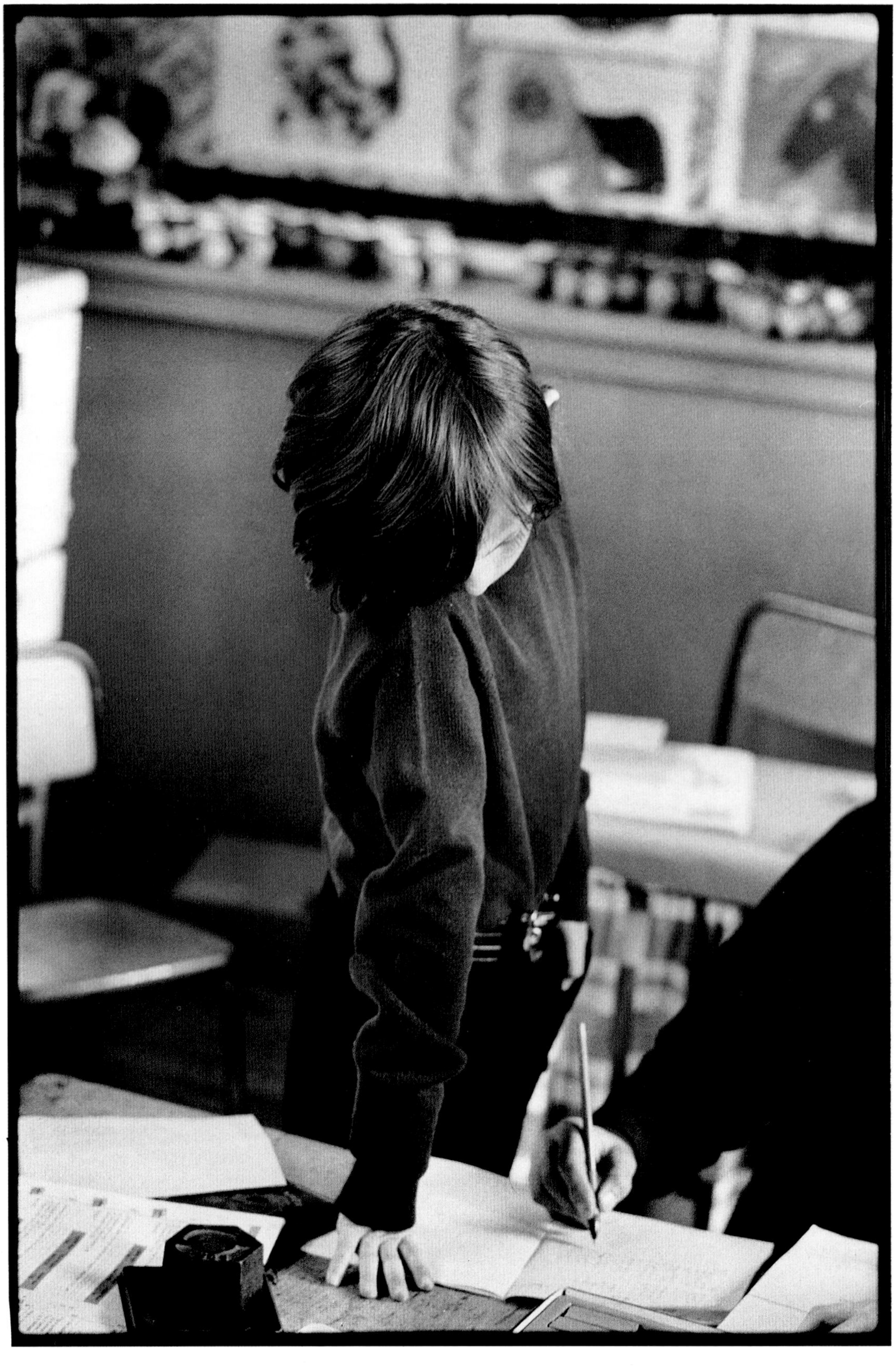

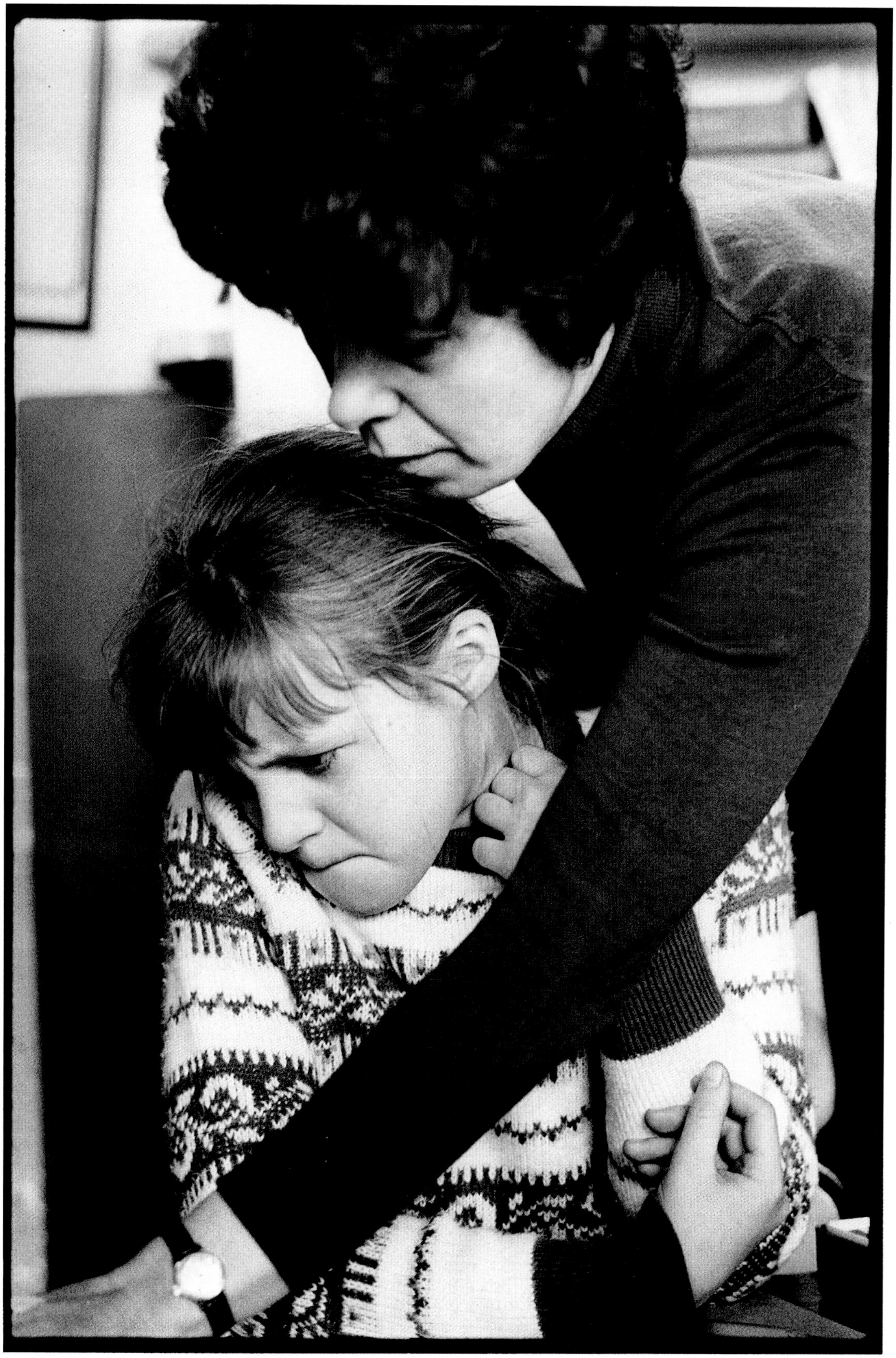

22

23

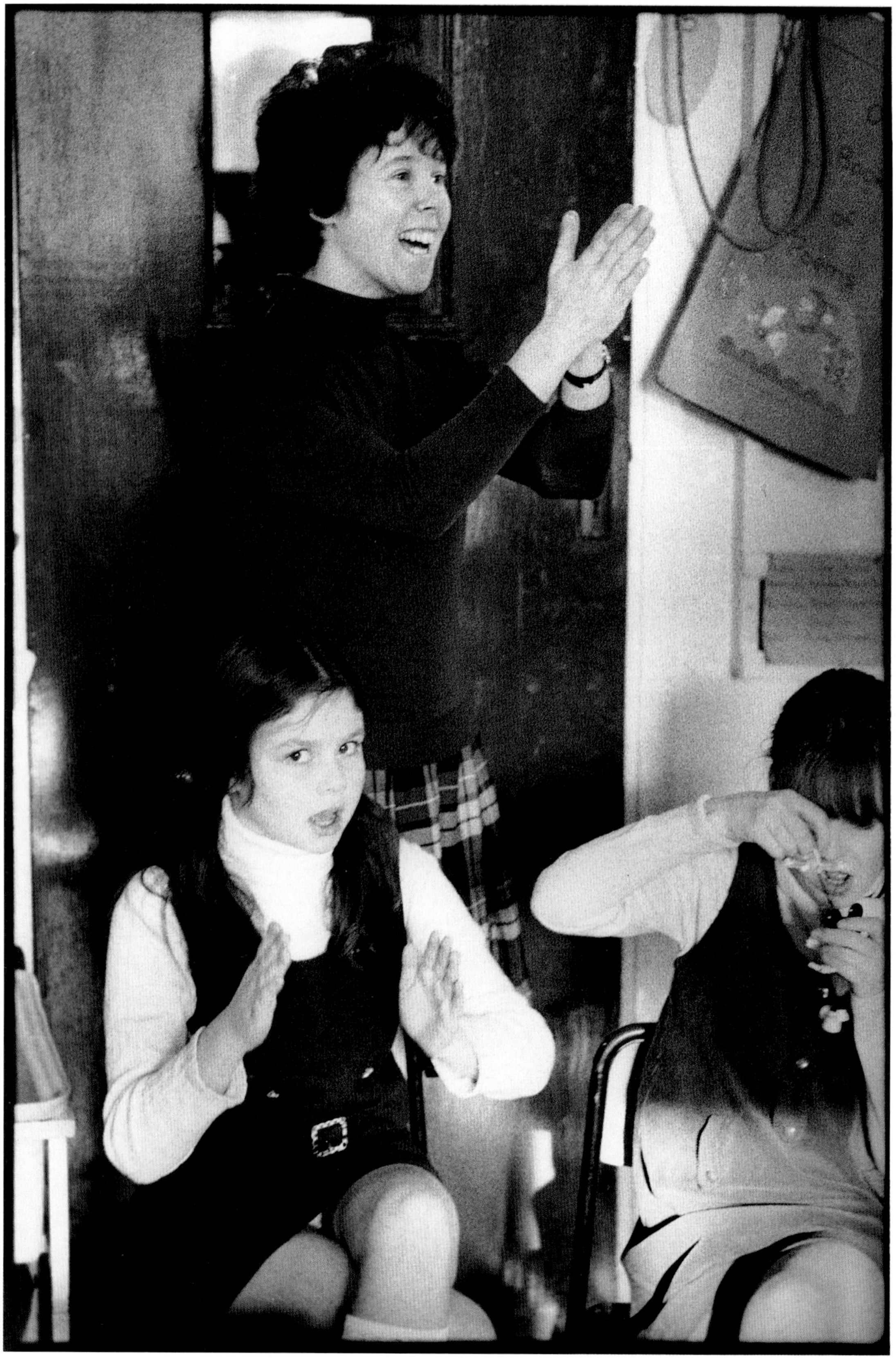

25

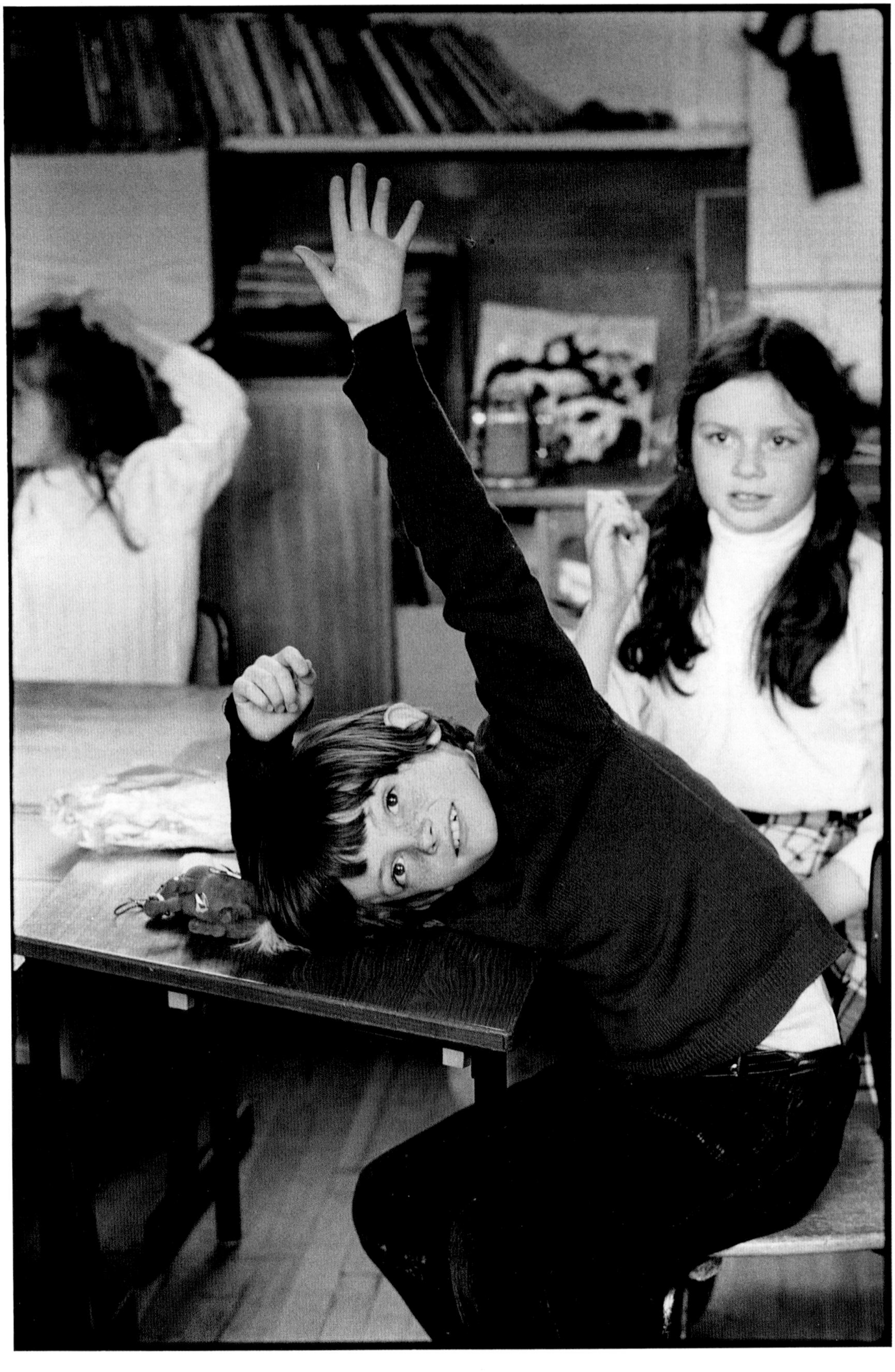

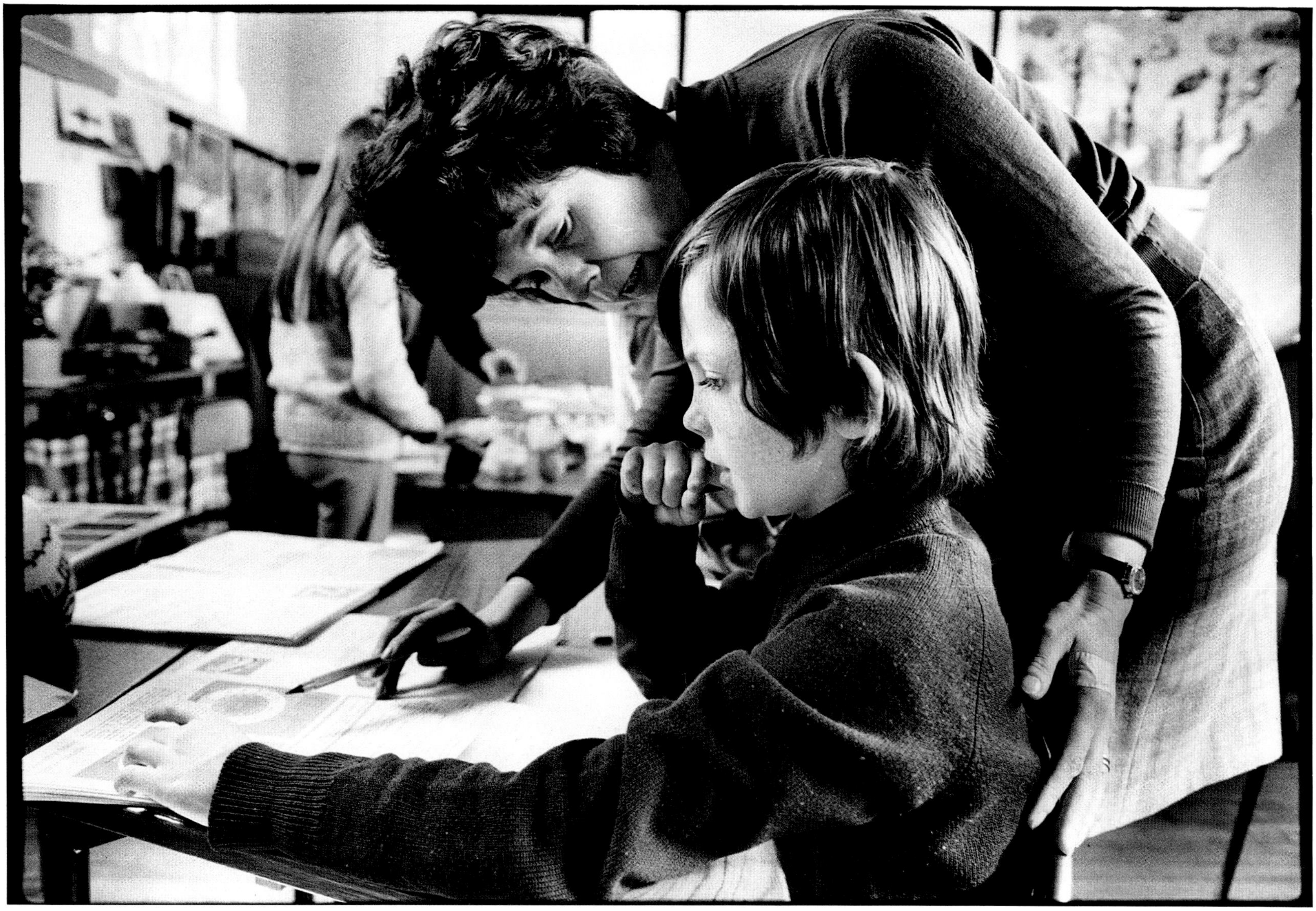

28

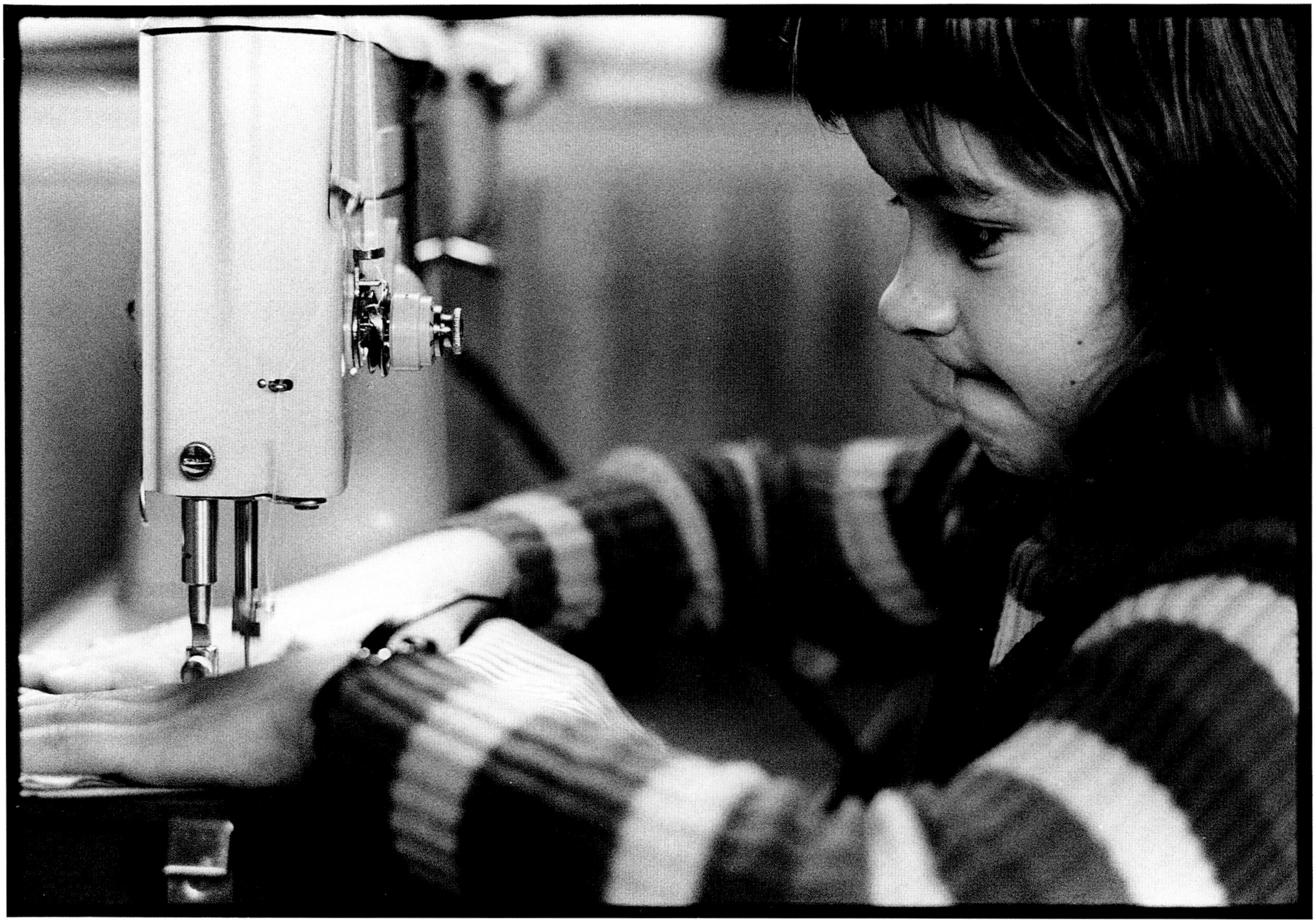

30

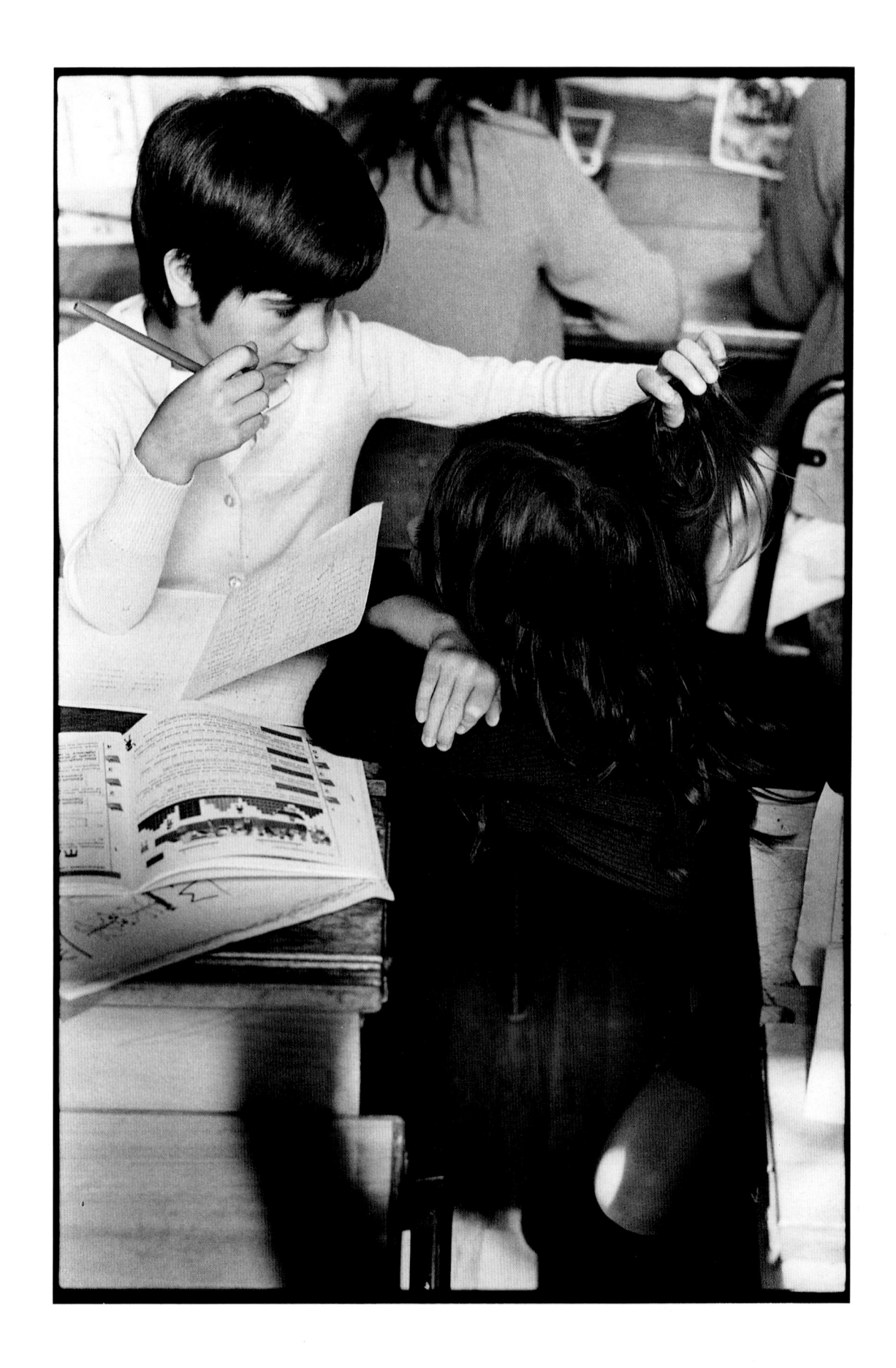

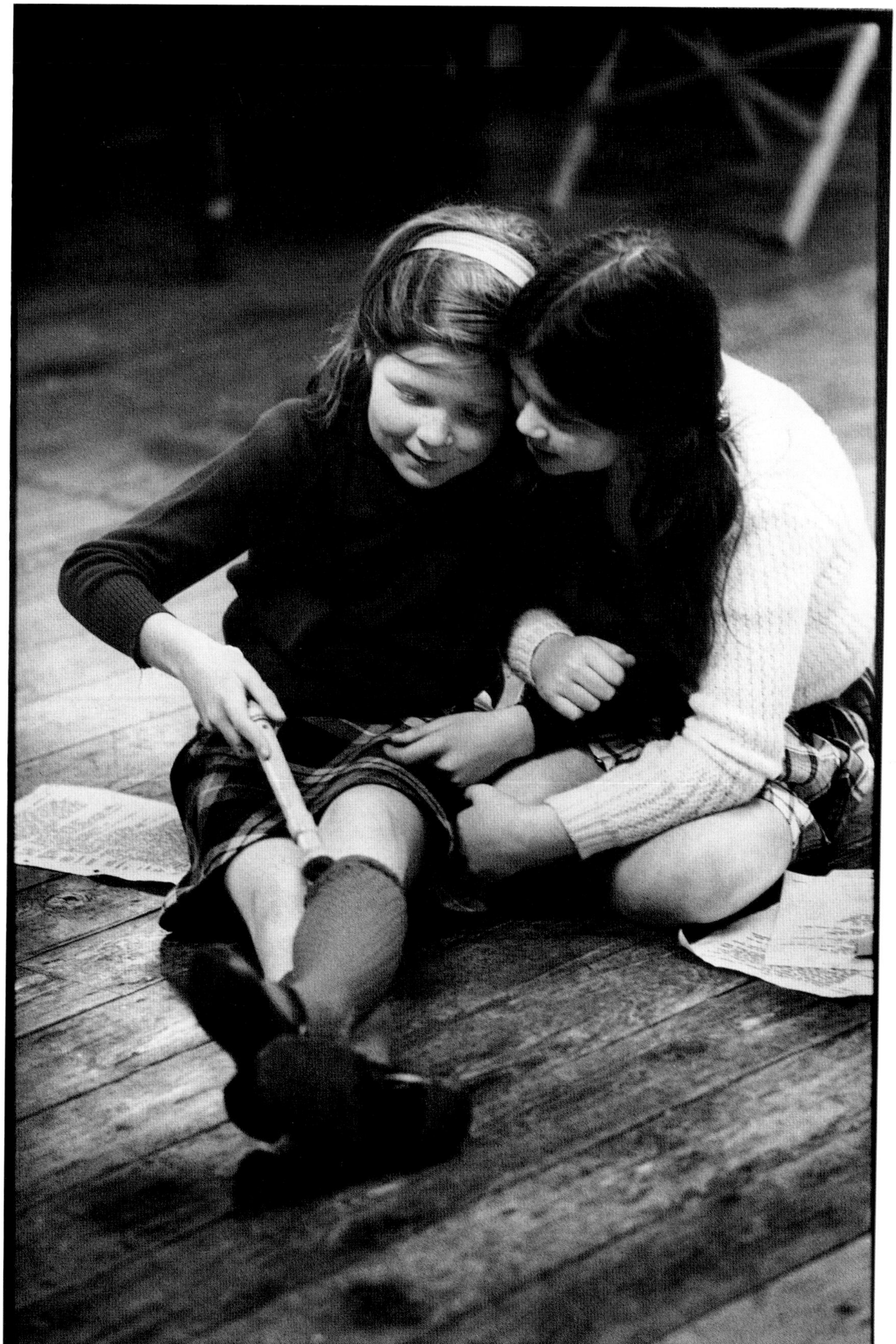

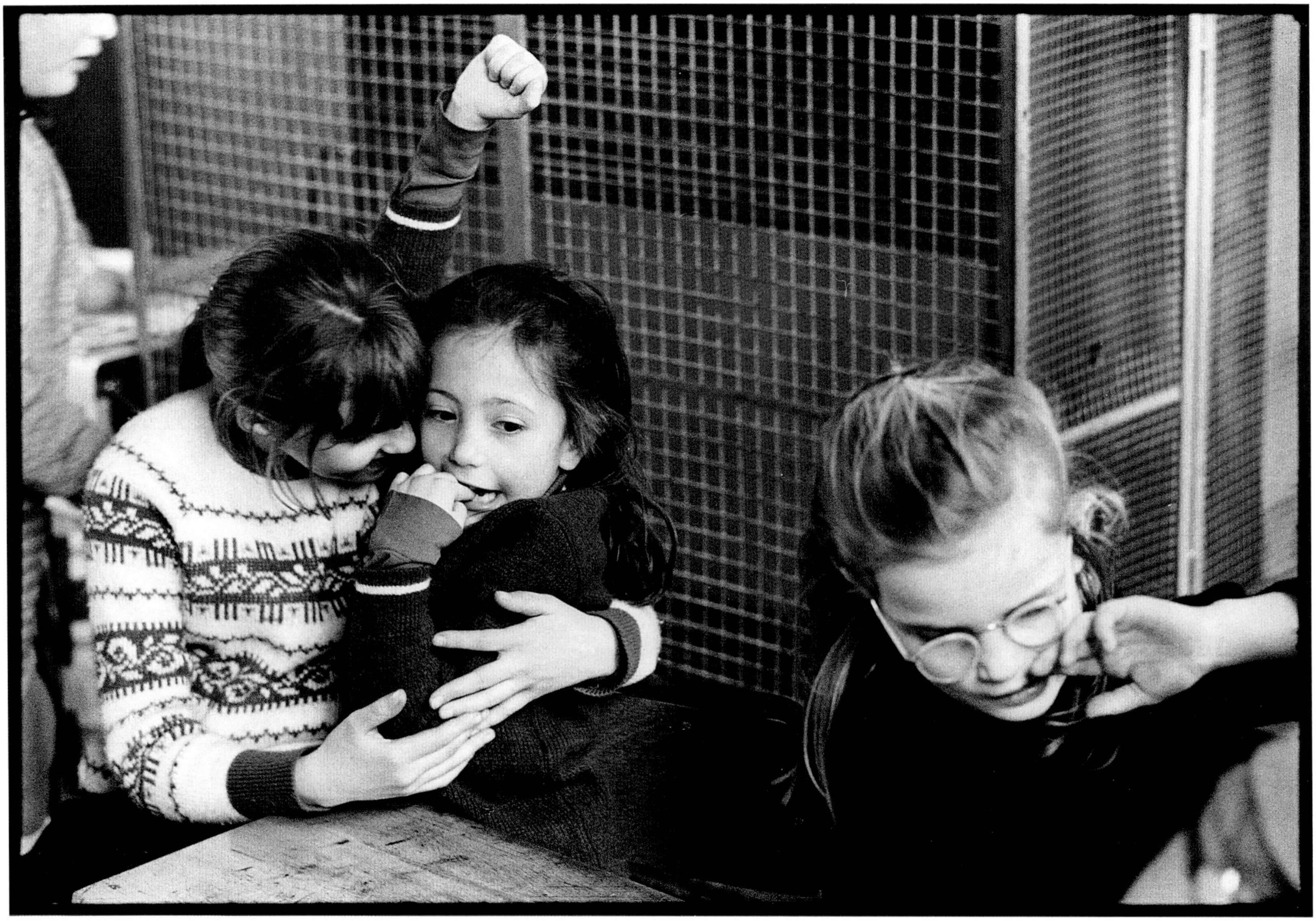

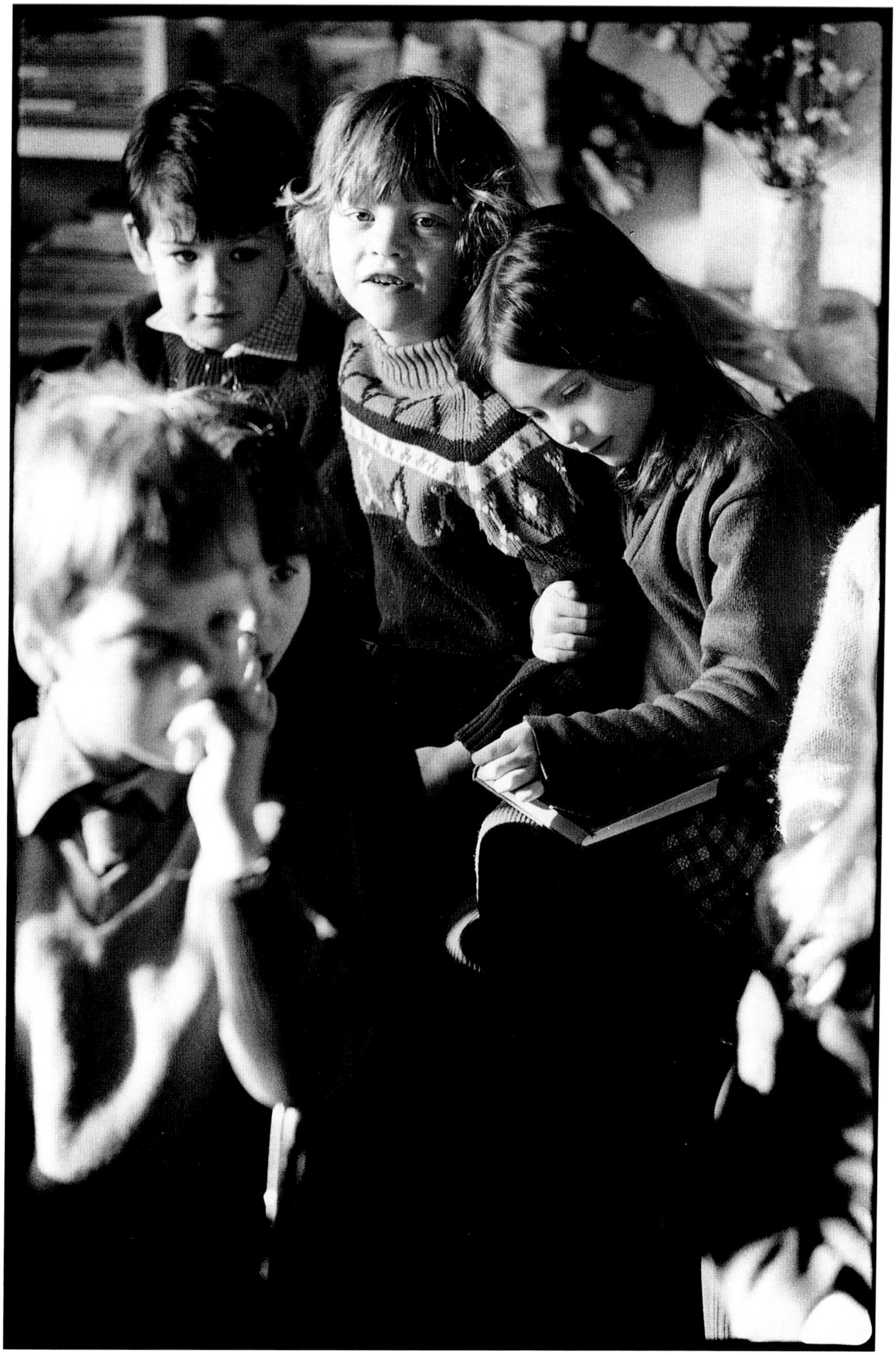

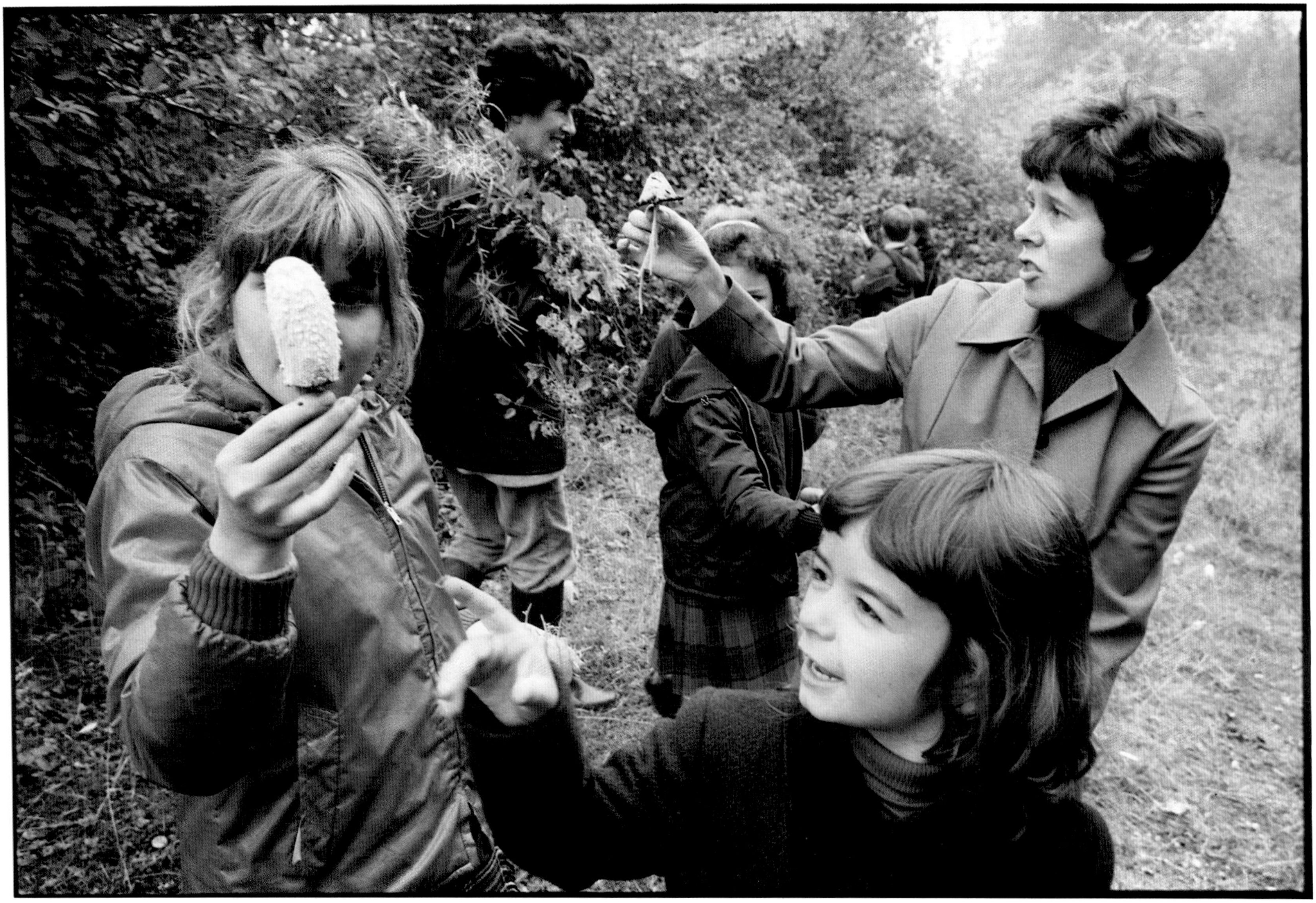

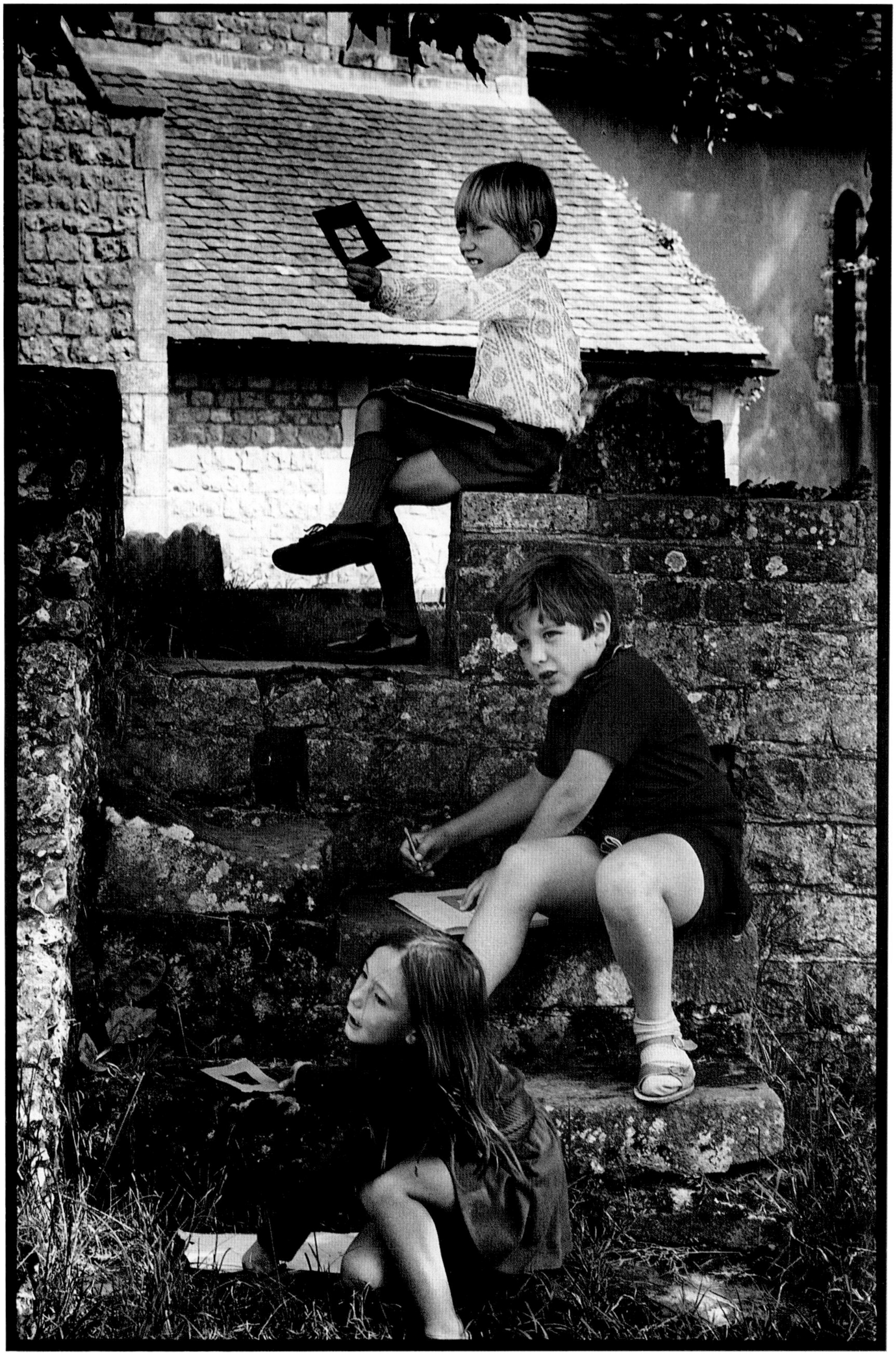

36

37

38

39

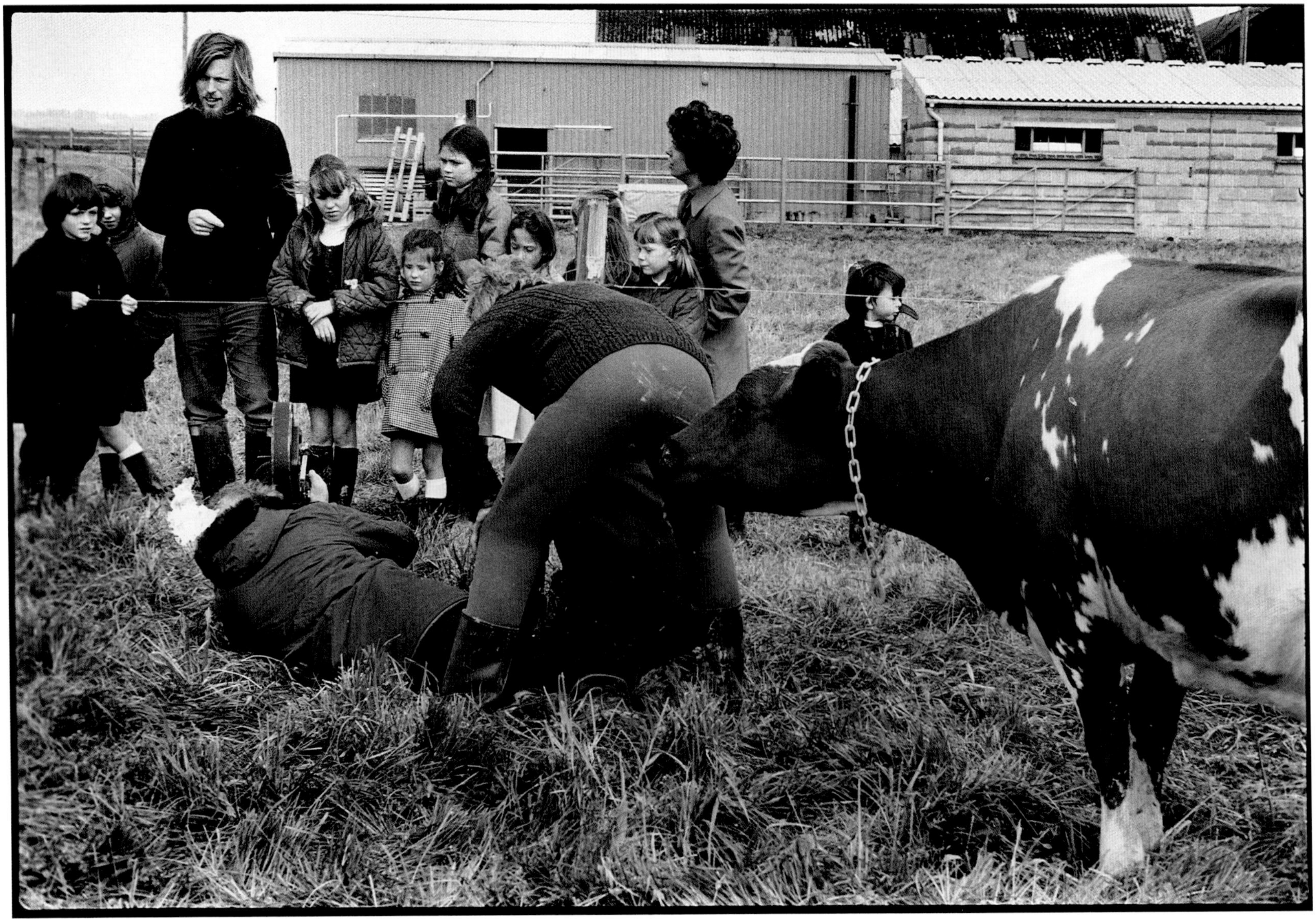

41

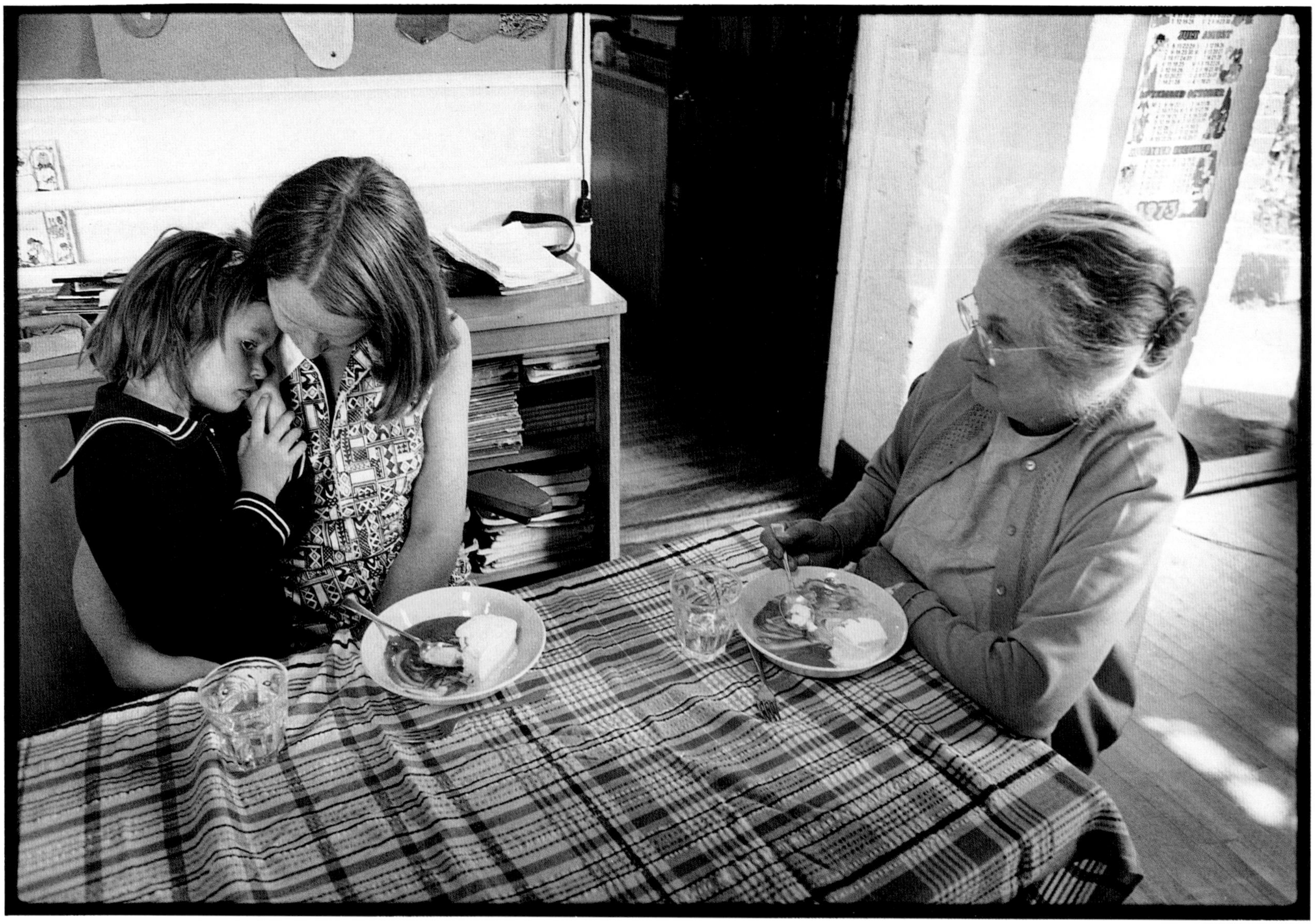

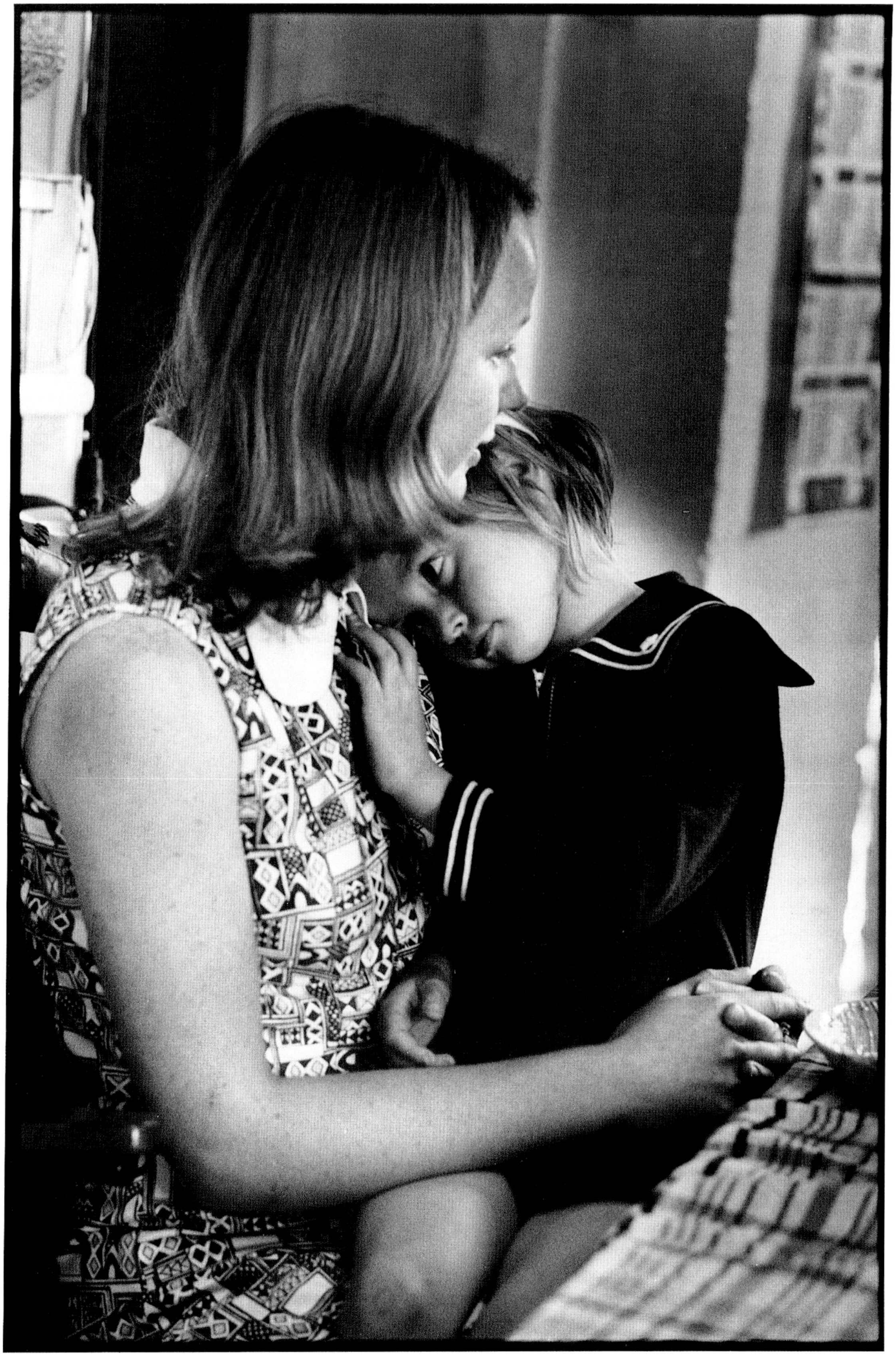

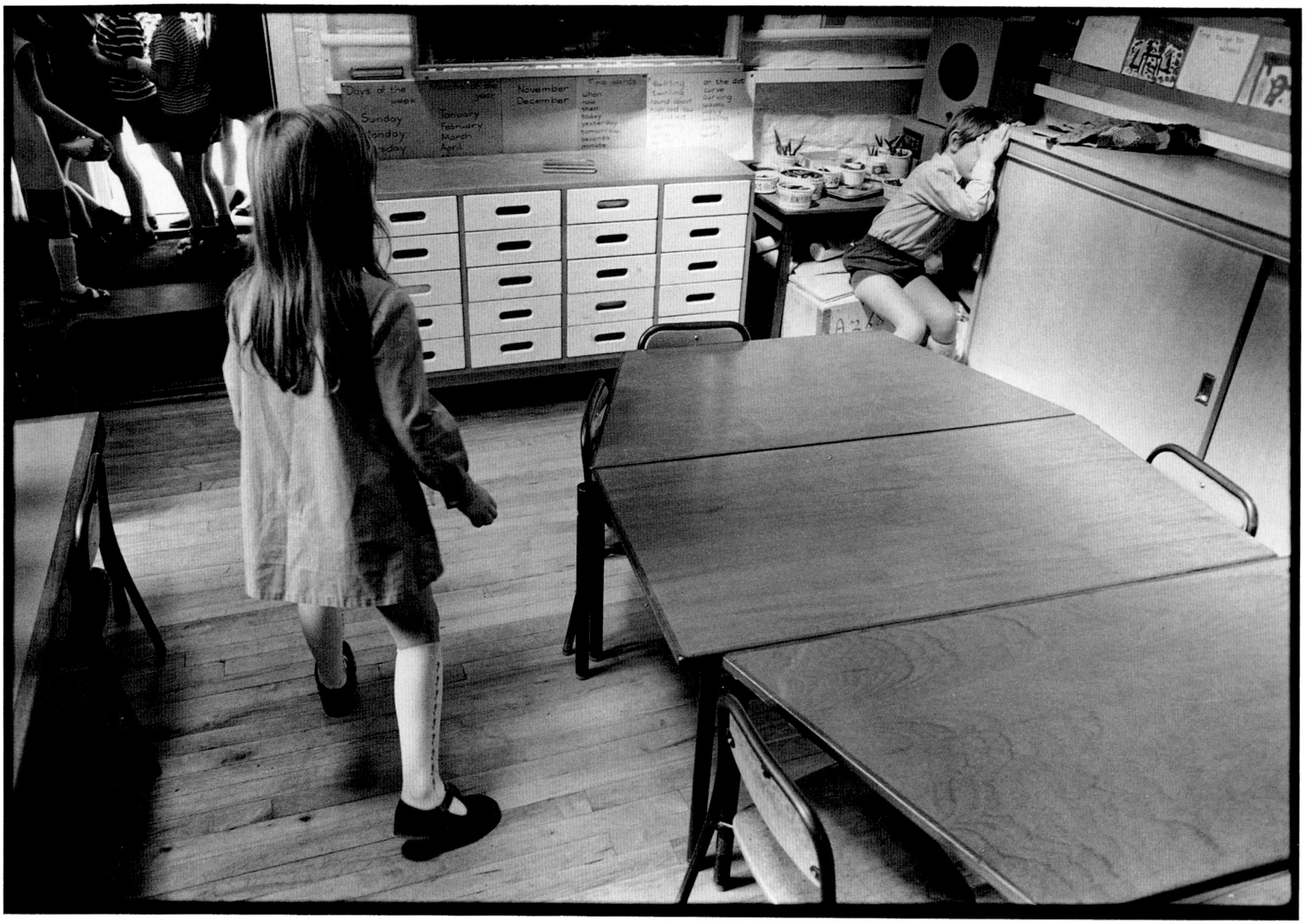

45

46

47

48

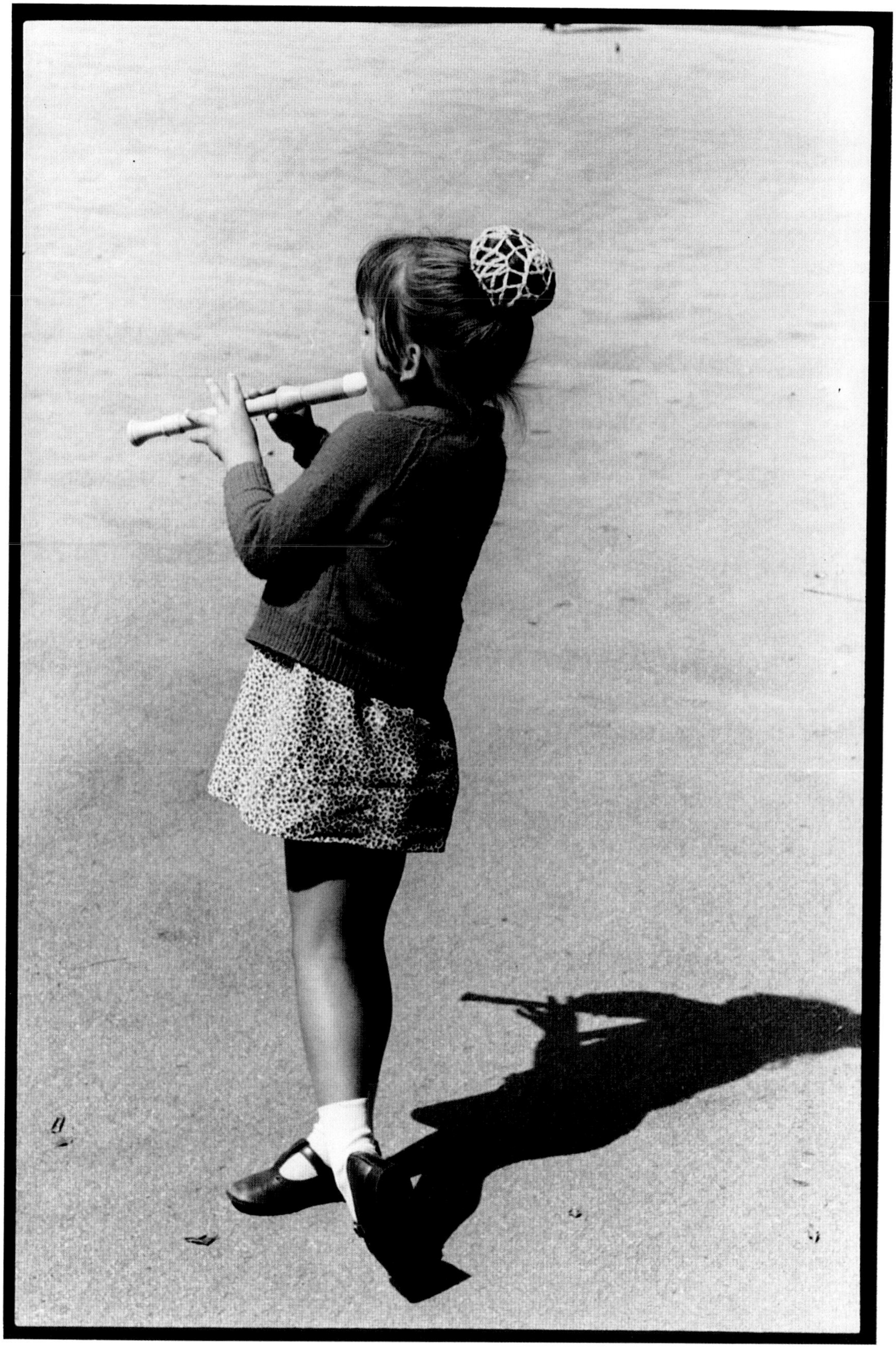

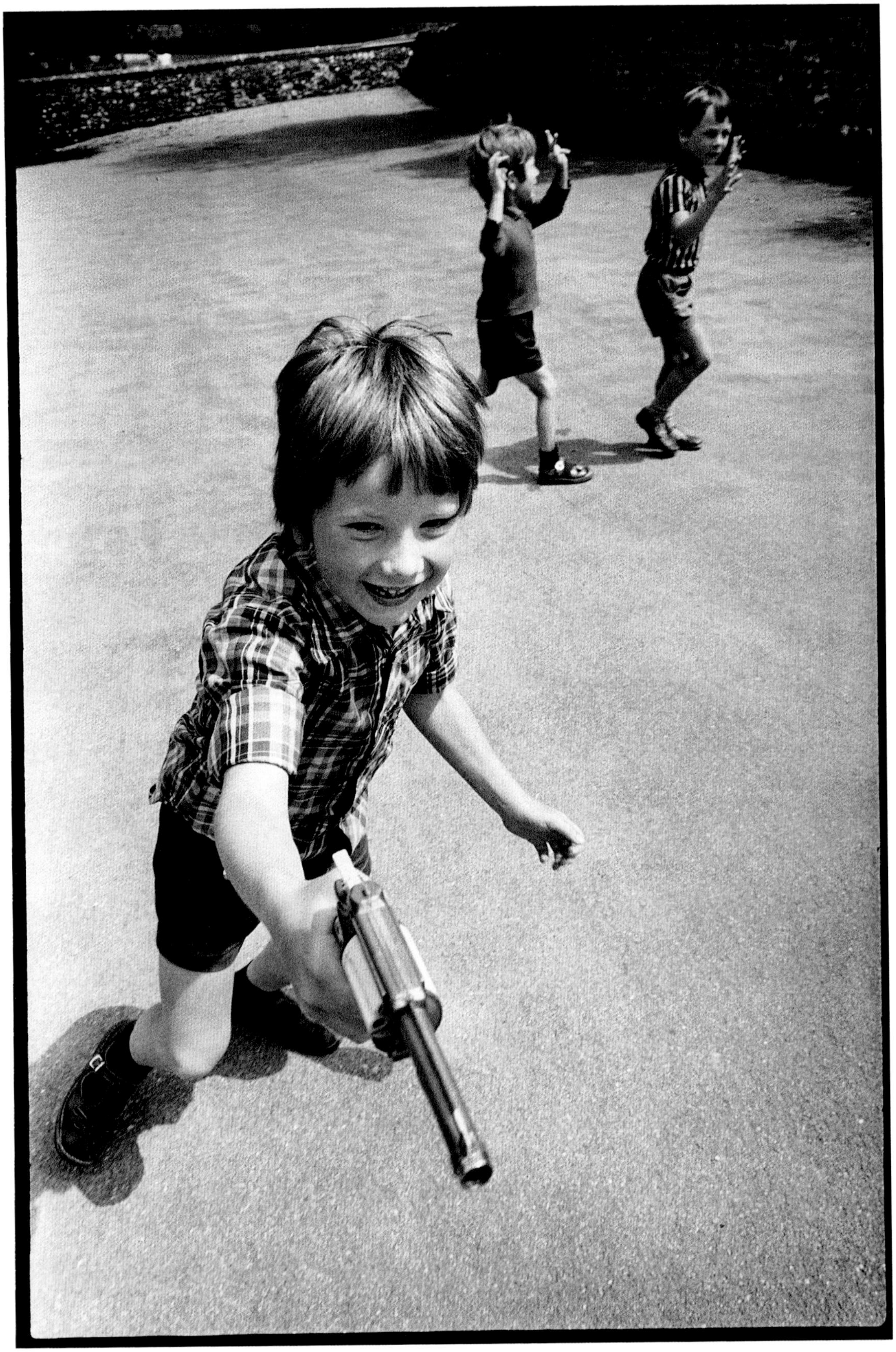

51

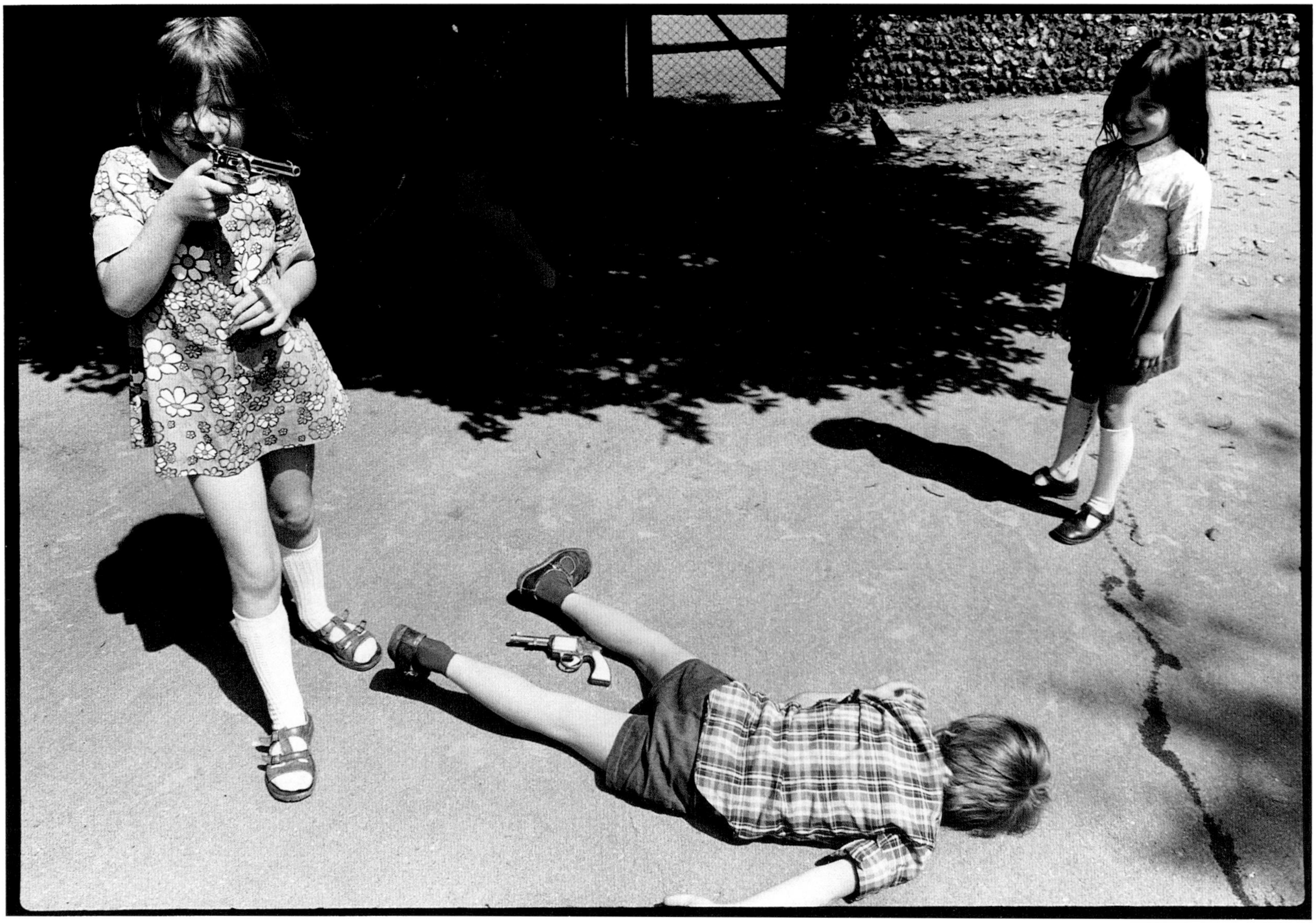

53

54

55

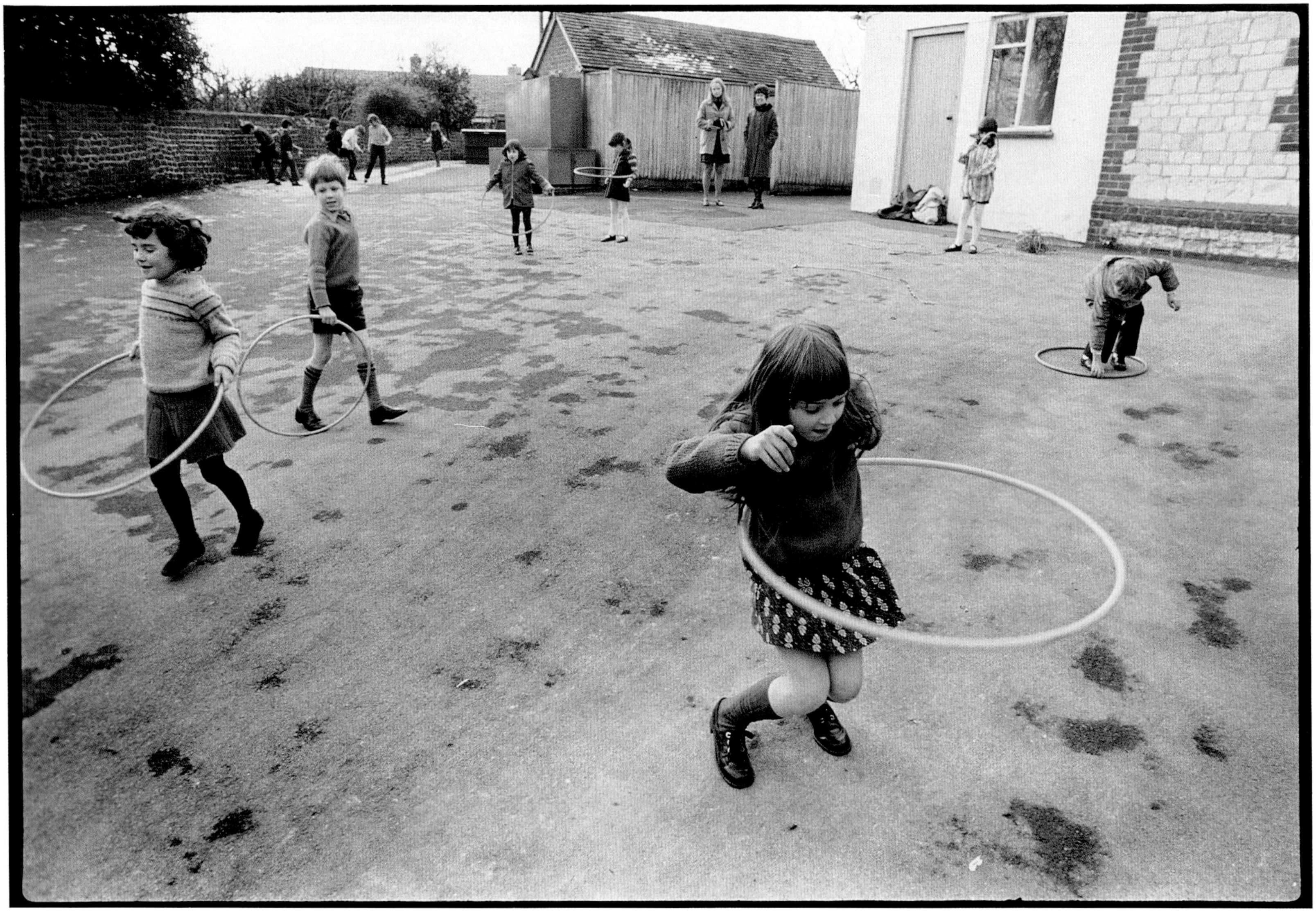

57

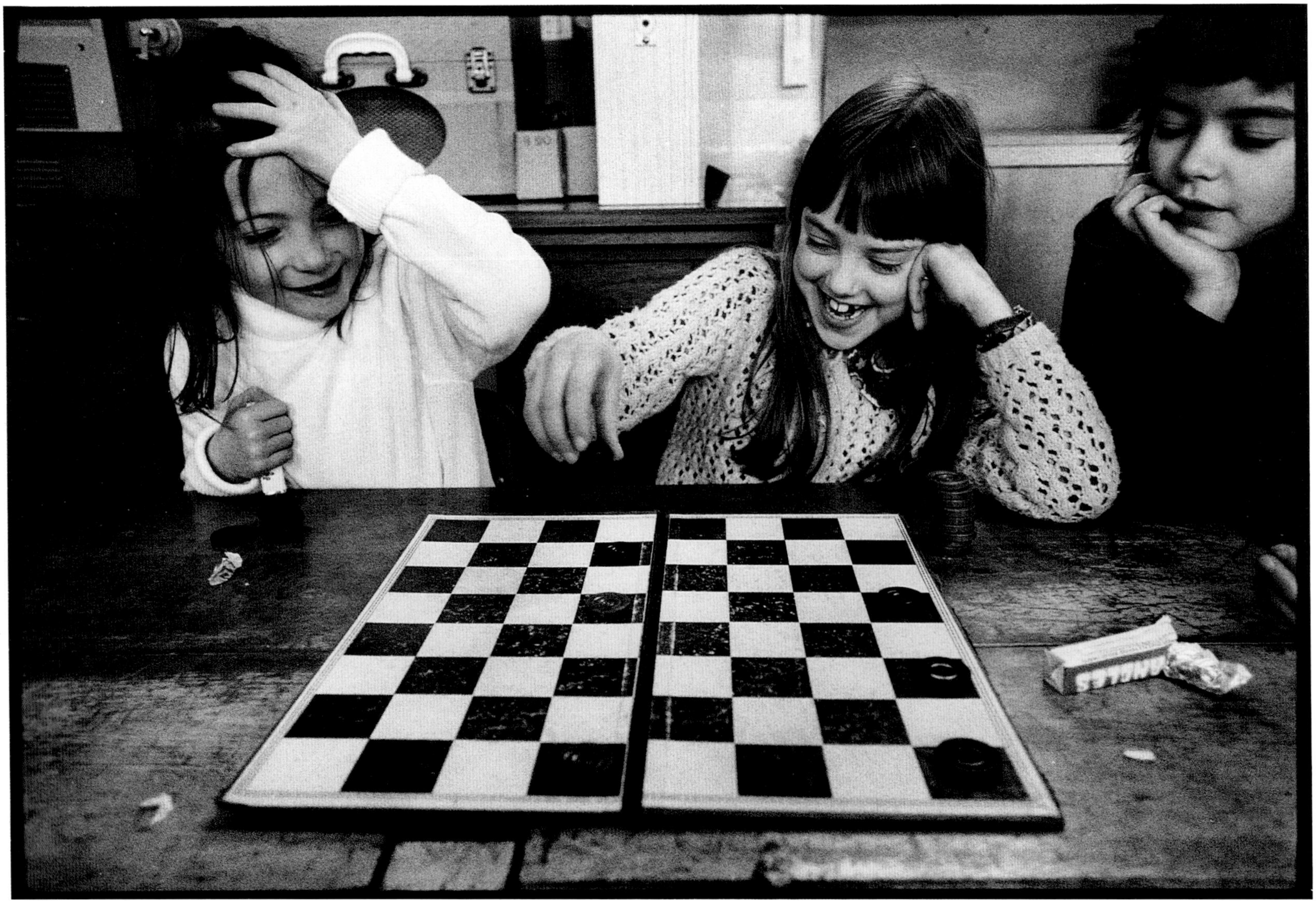

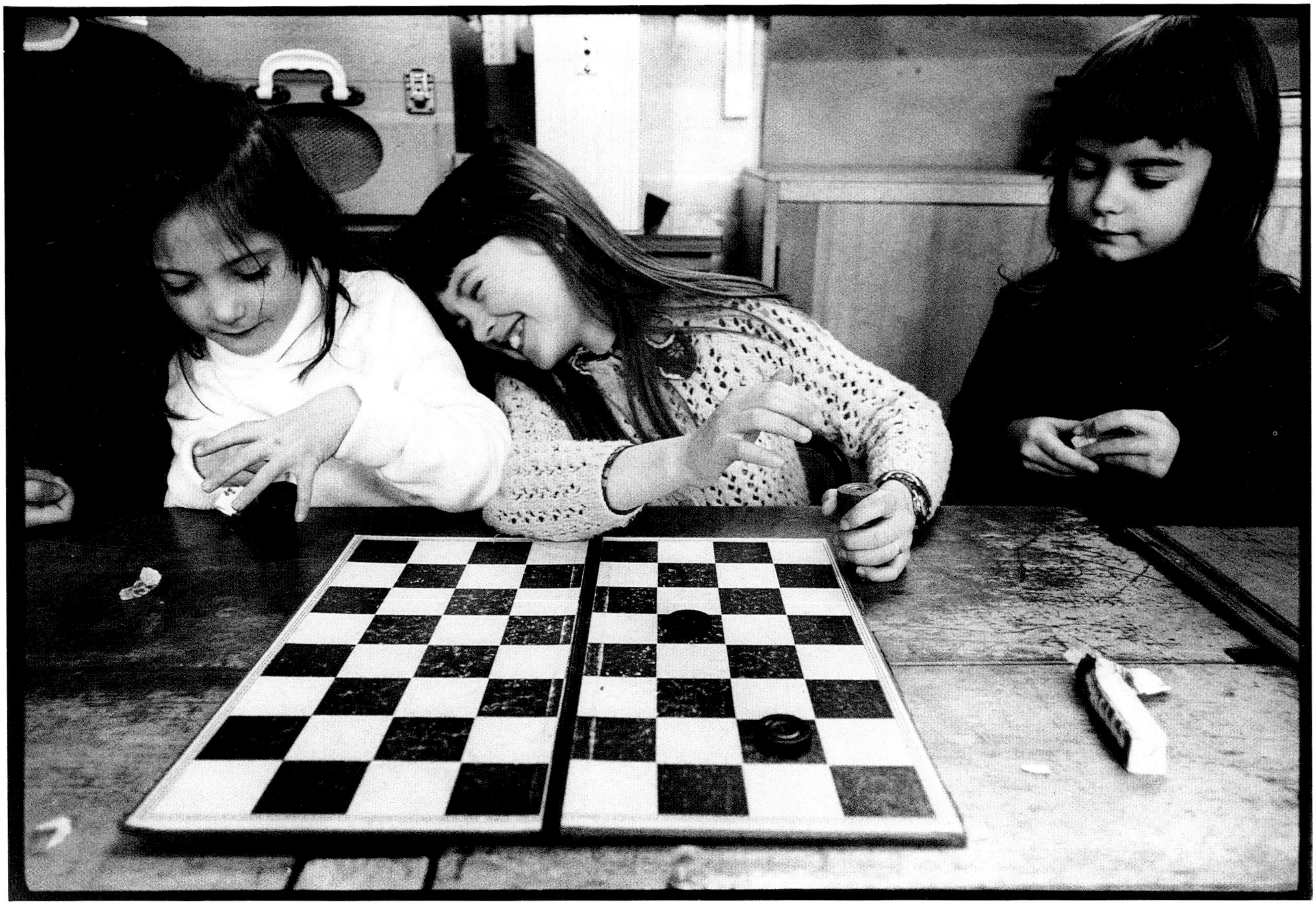

60

61

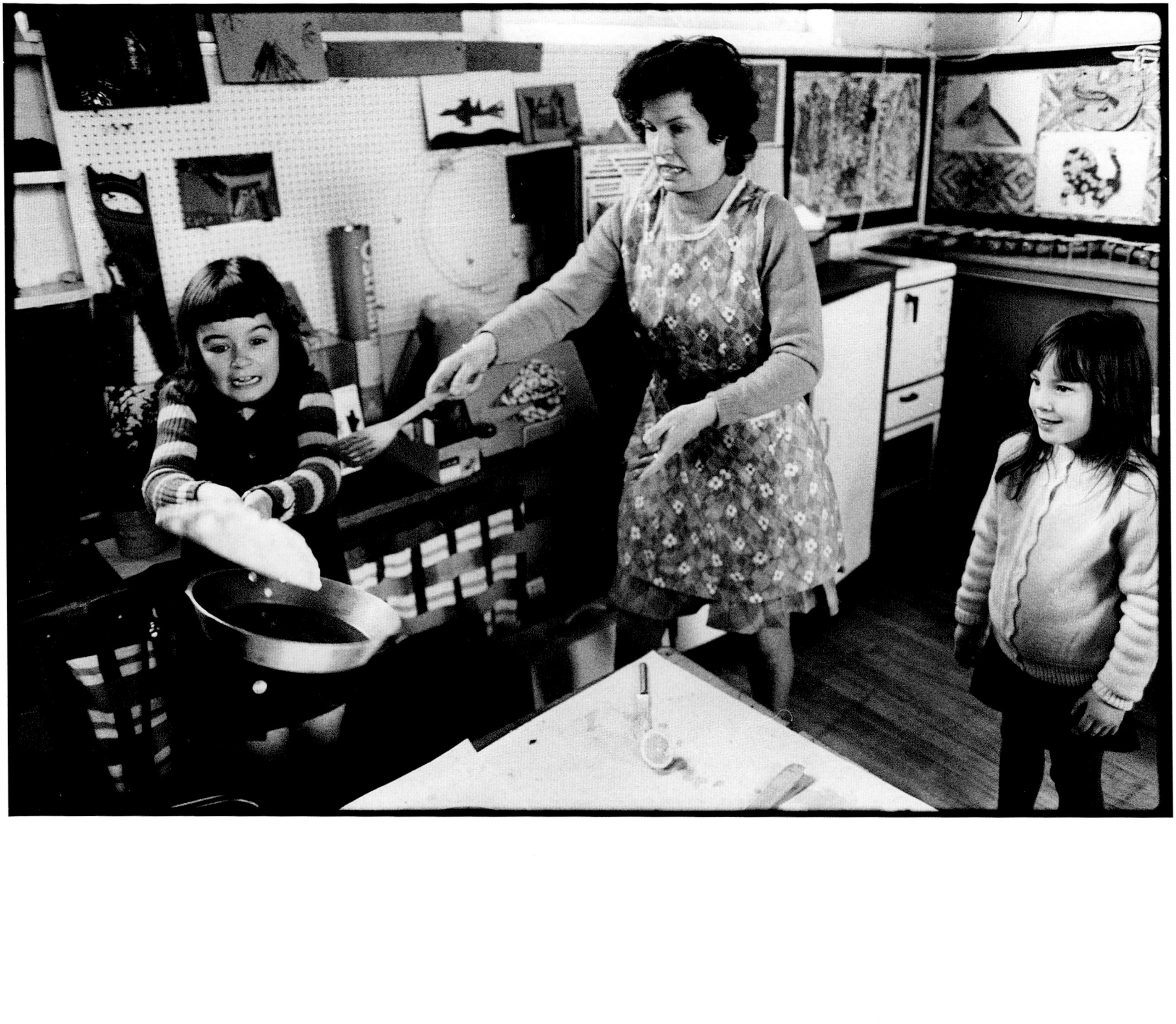

63

64

65

66

67

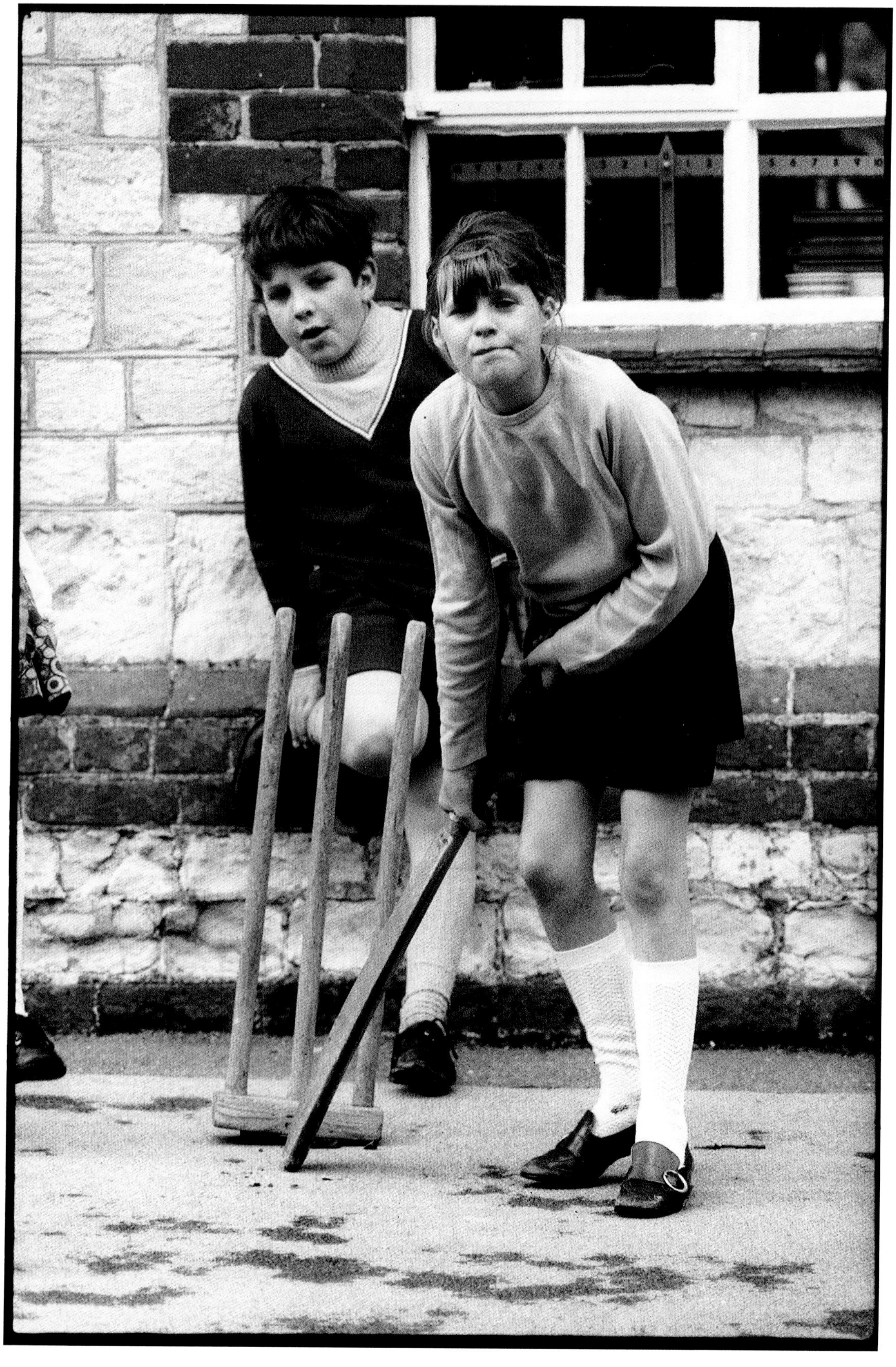

69

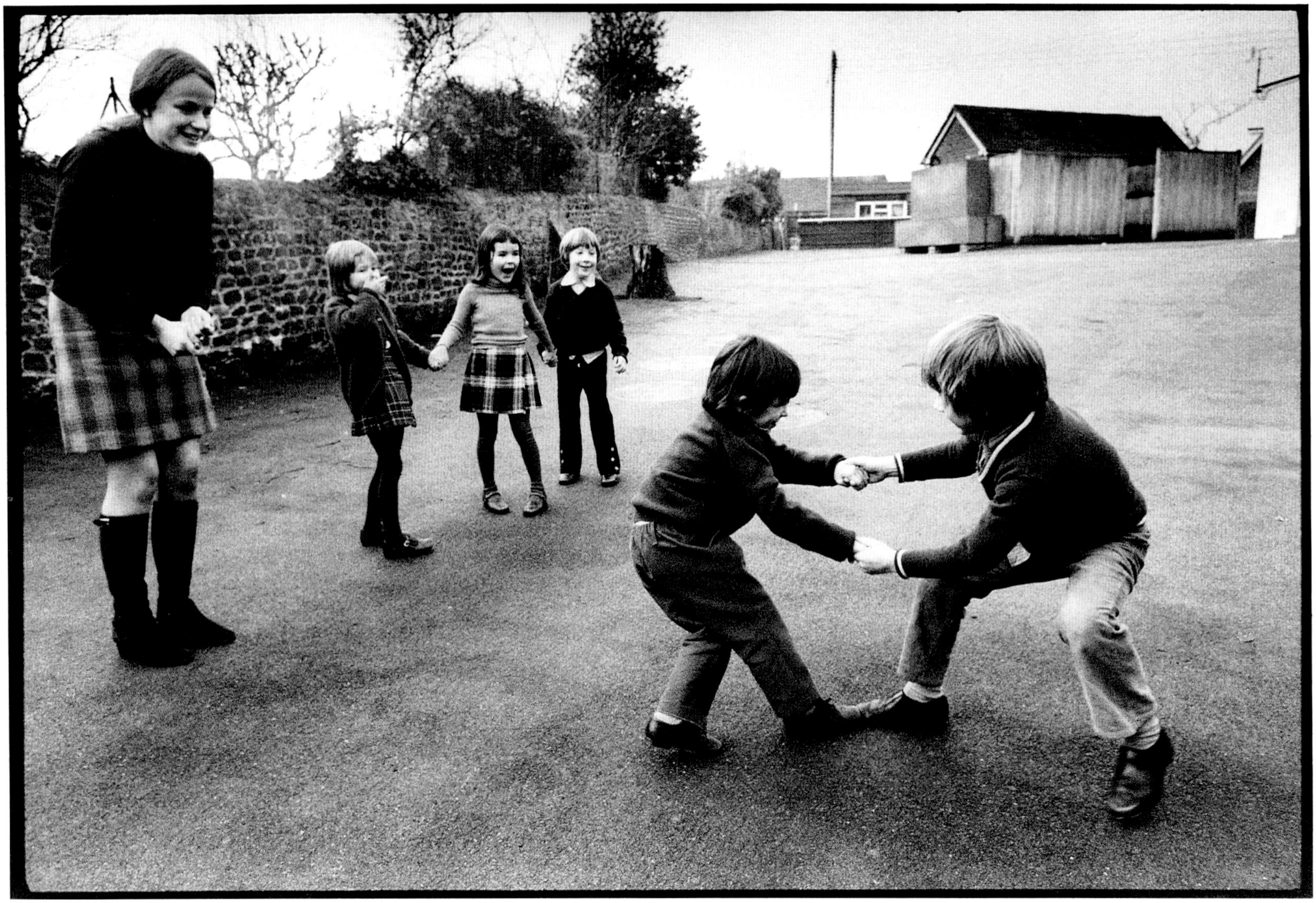

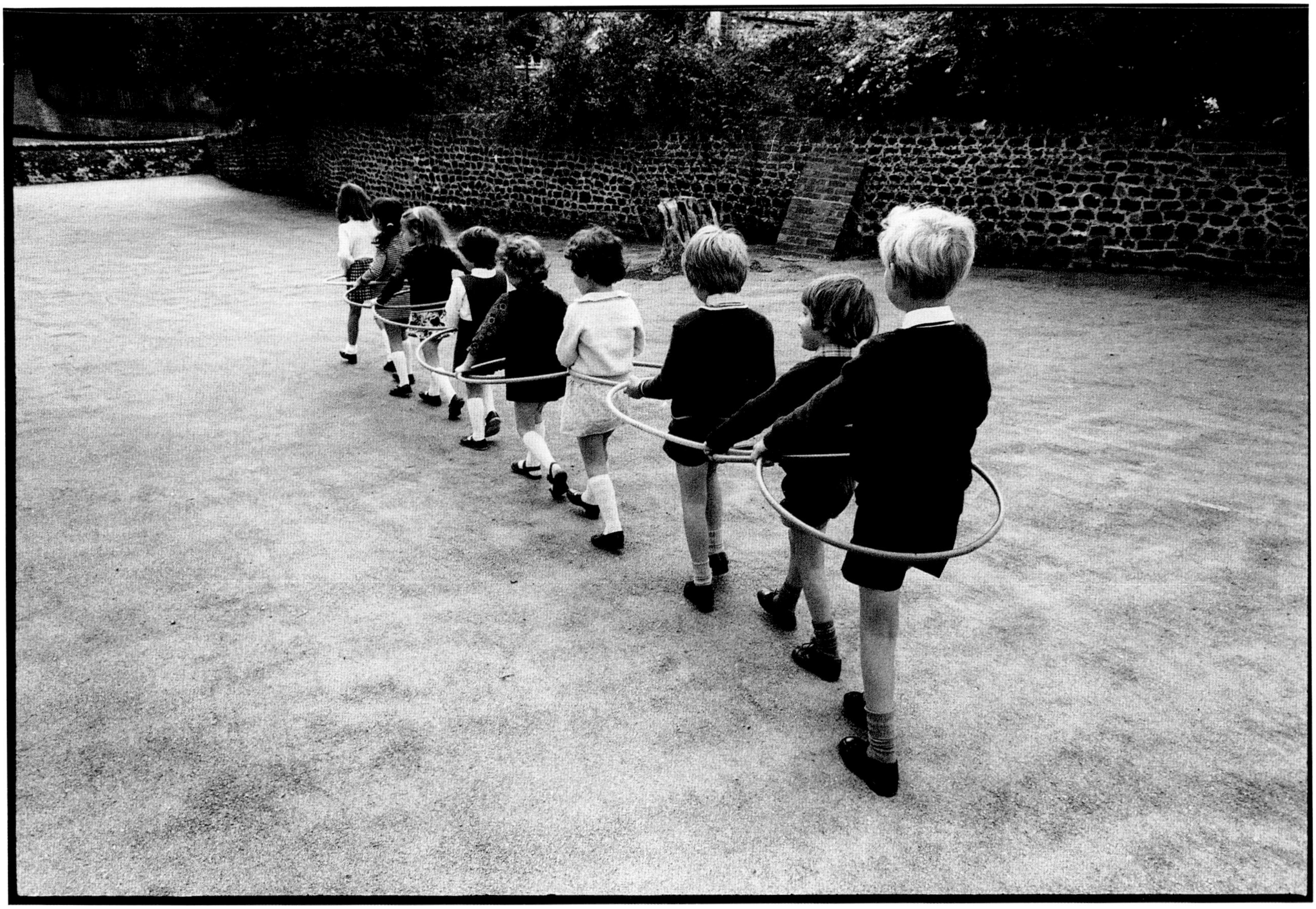

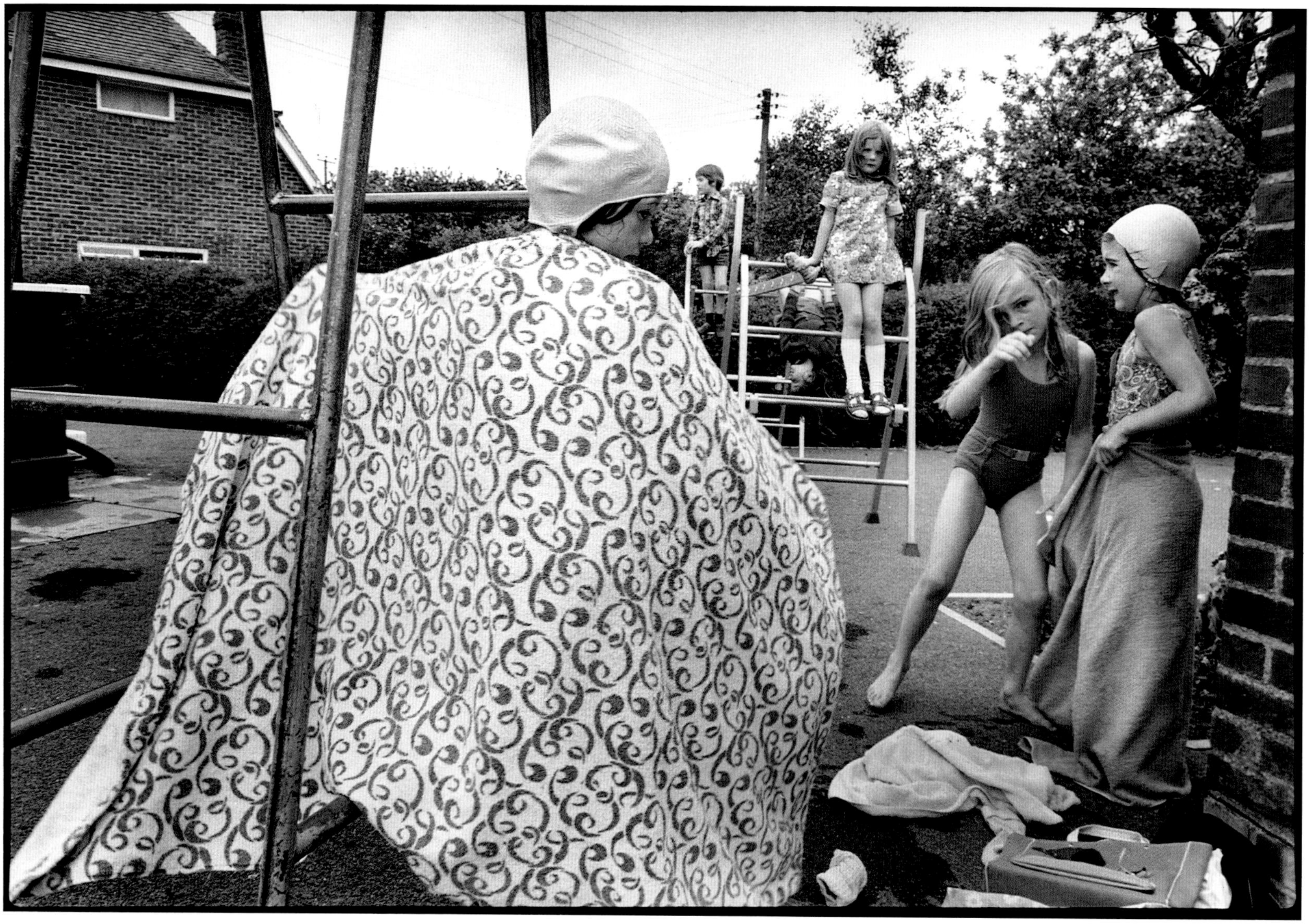

73

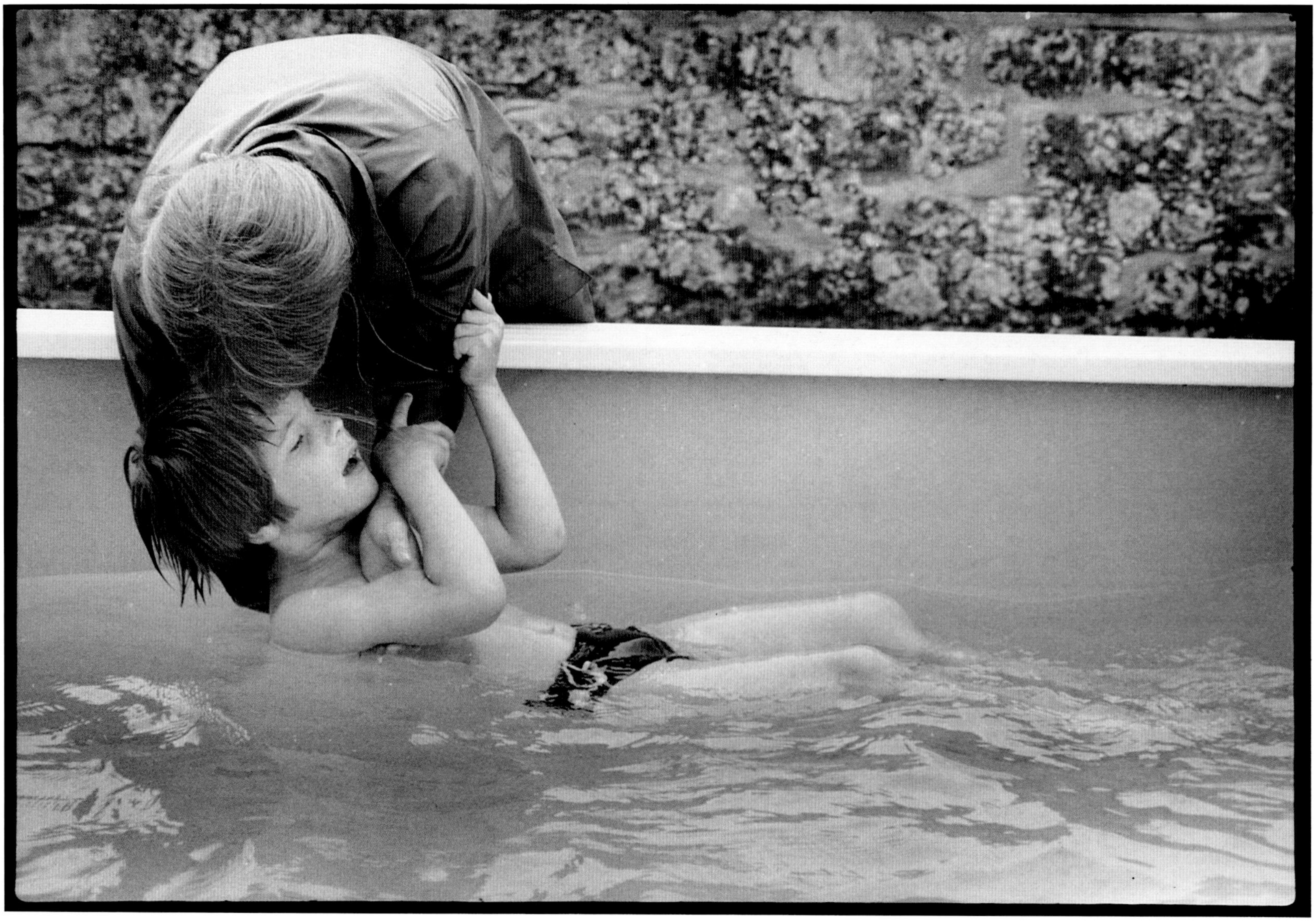

75

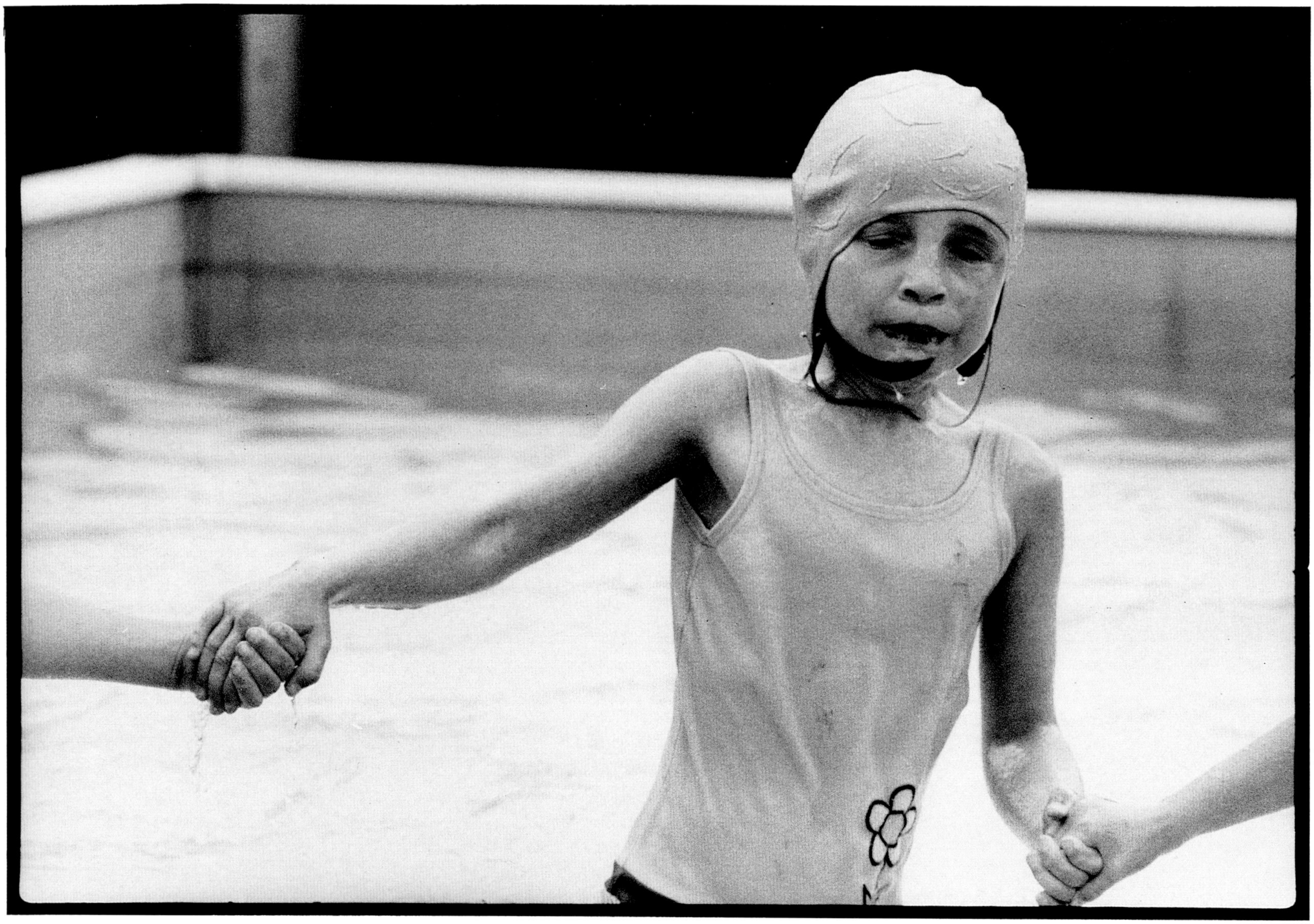

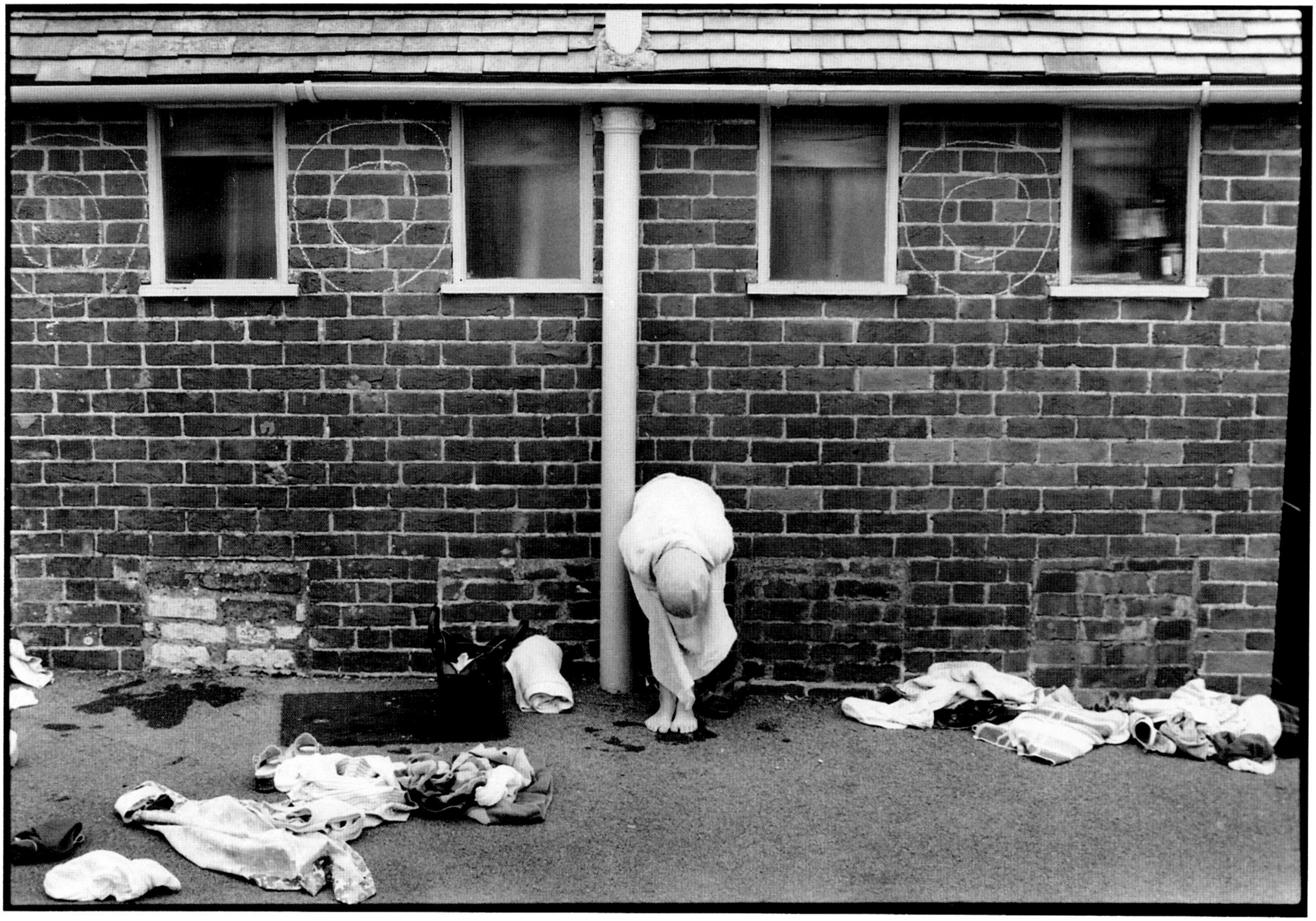

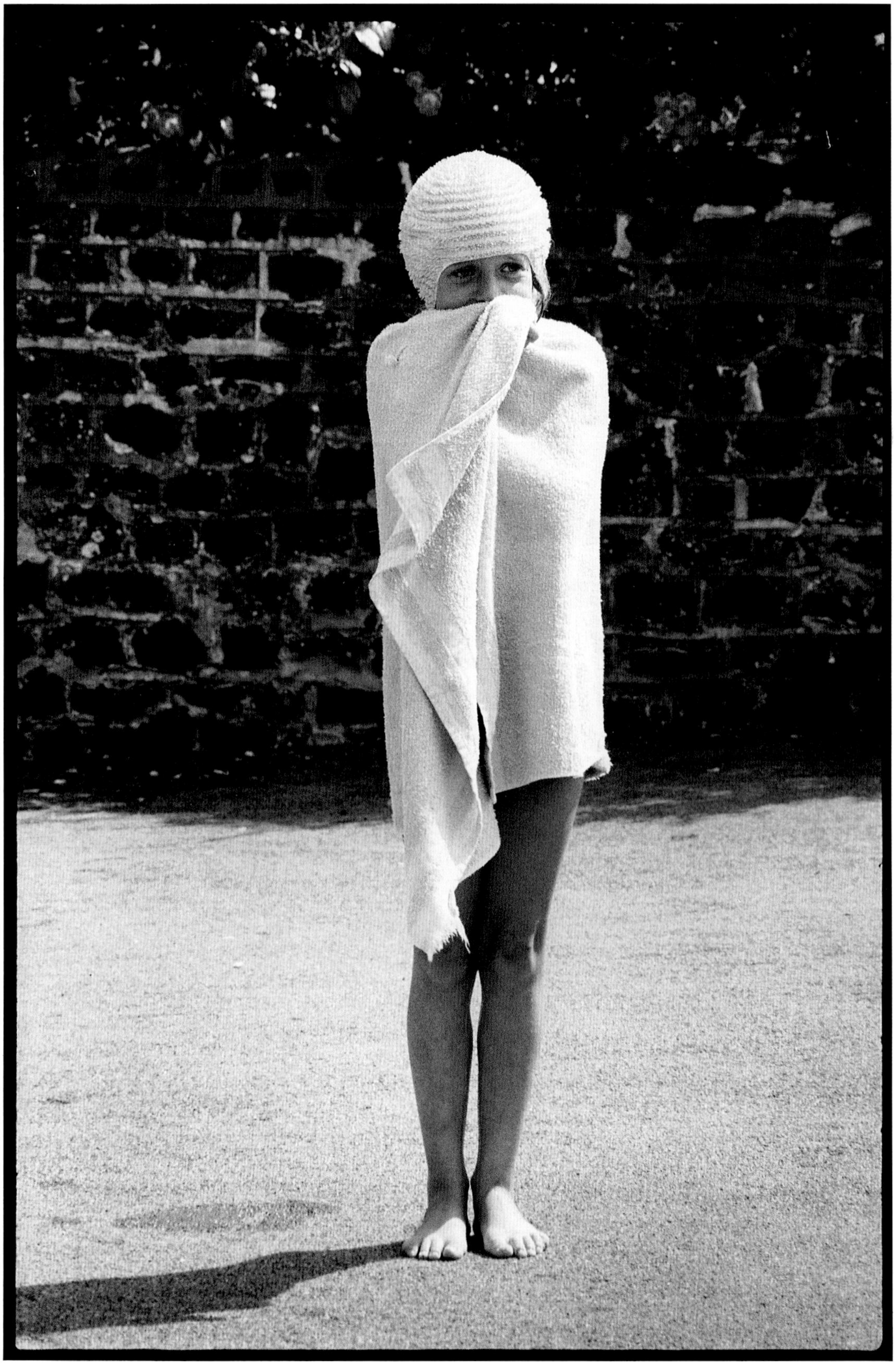

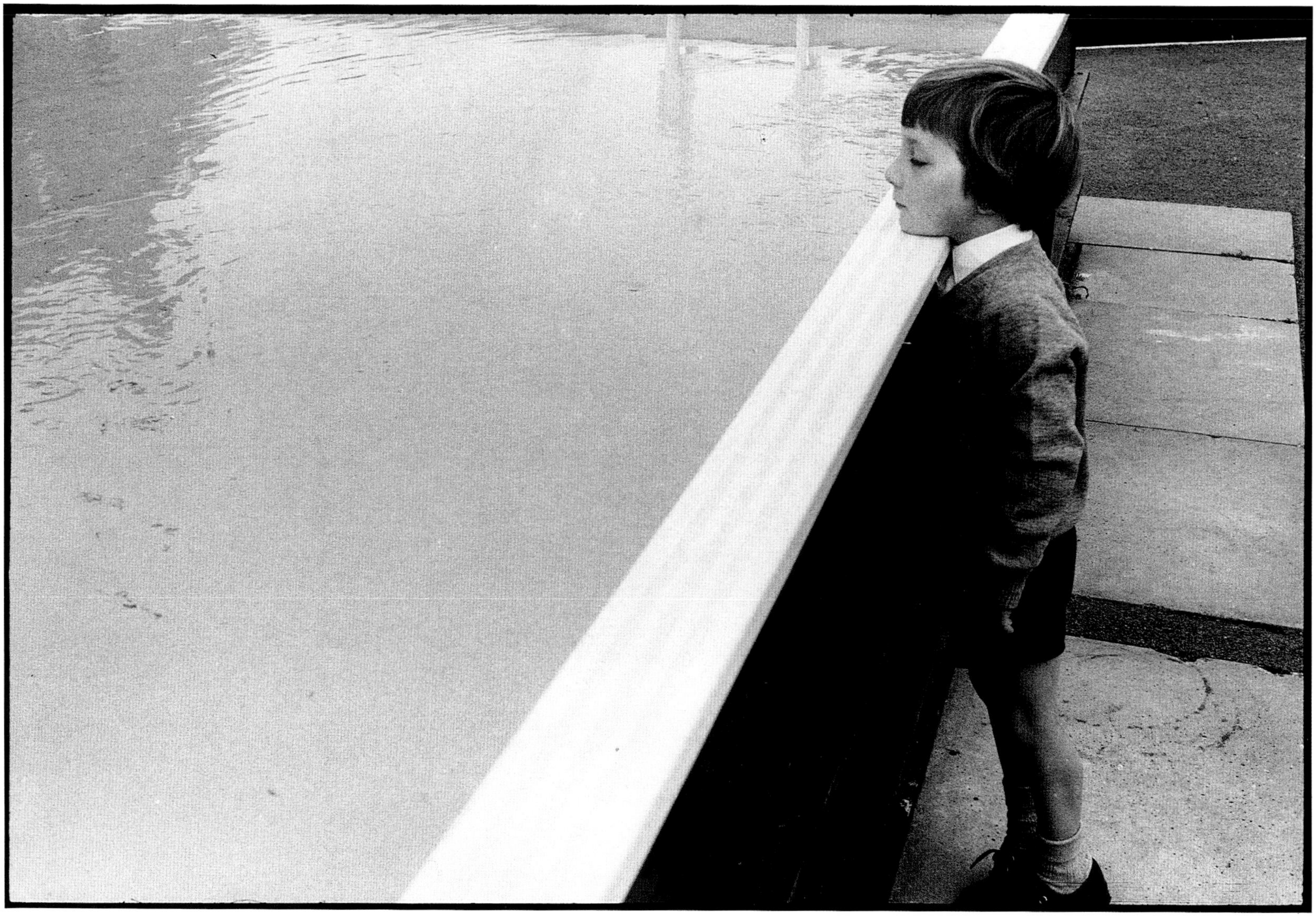

80

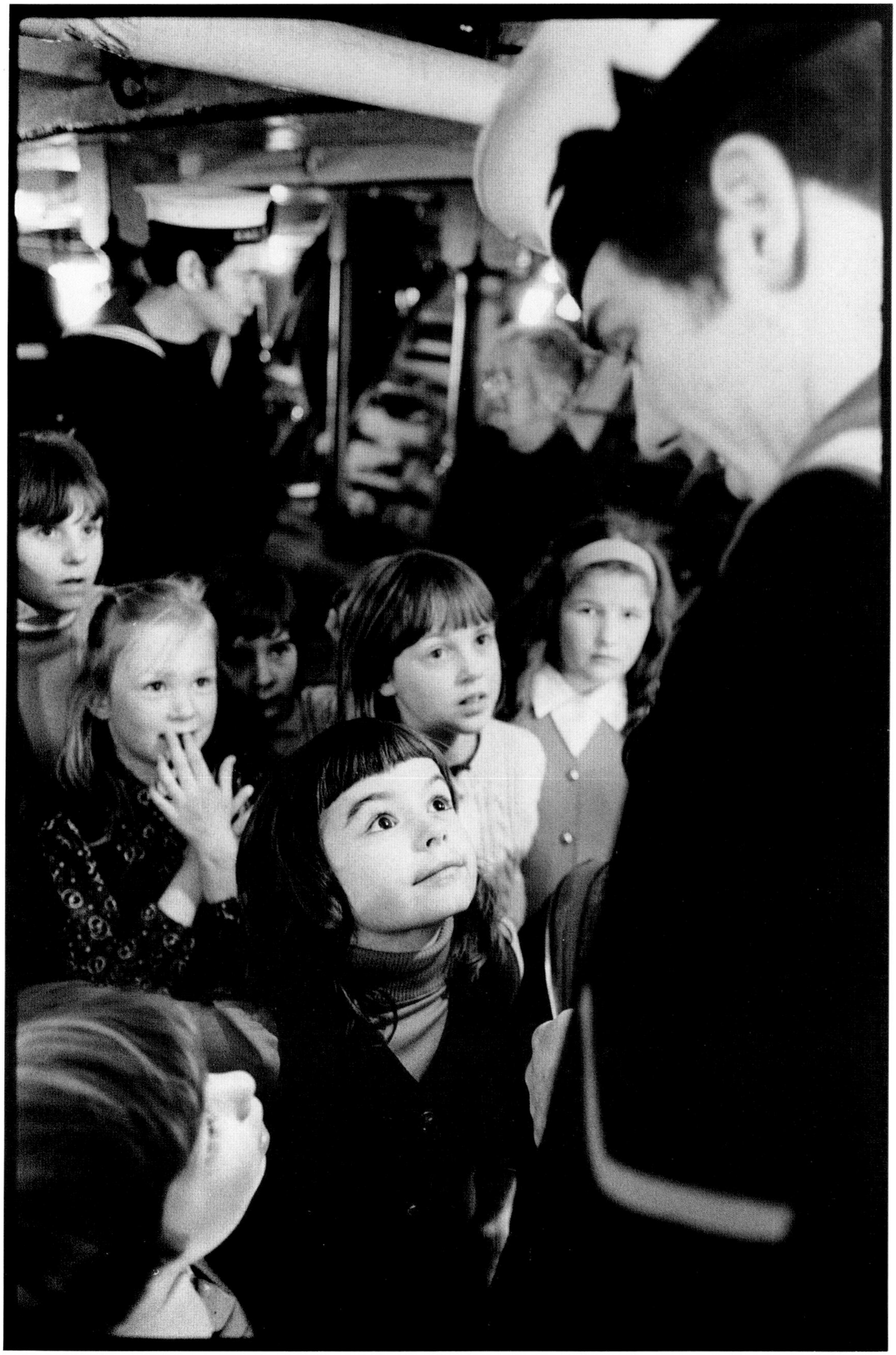

82

83

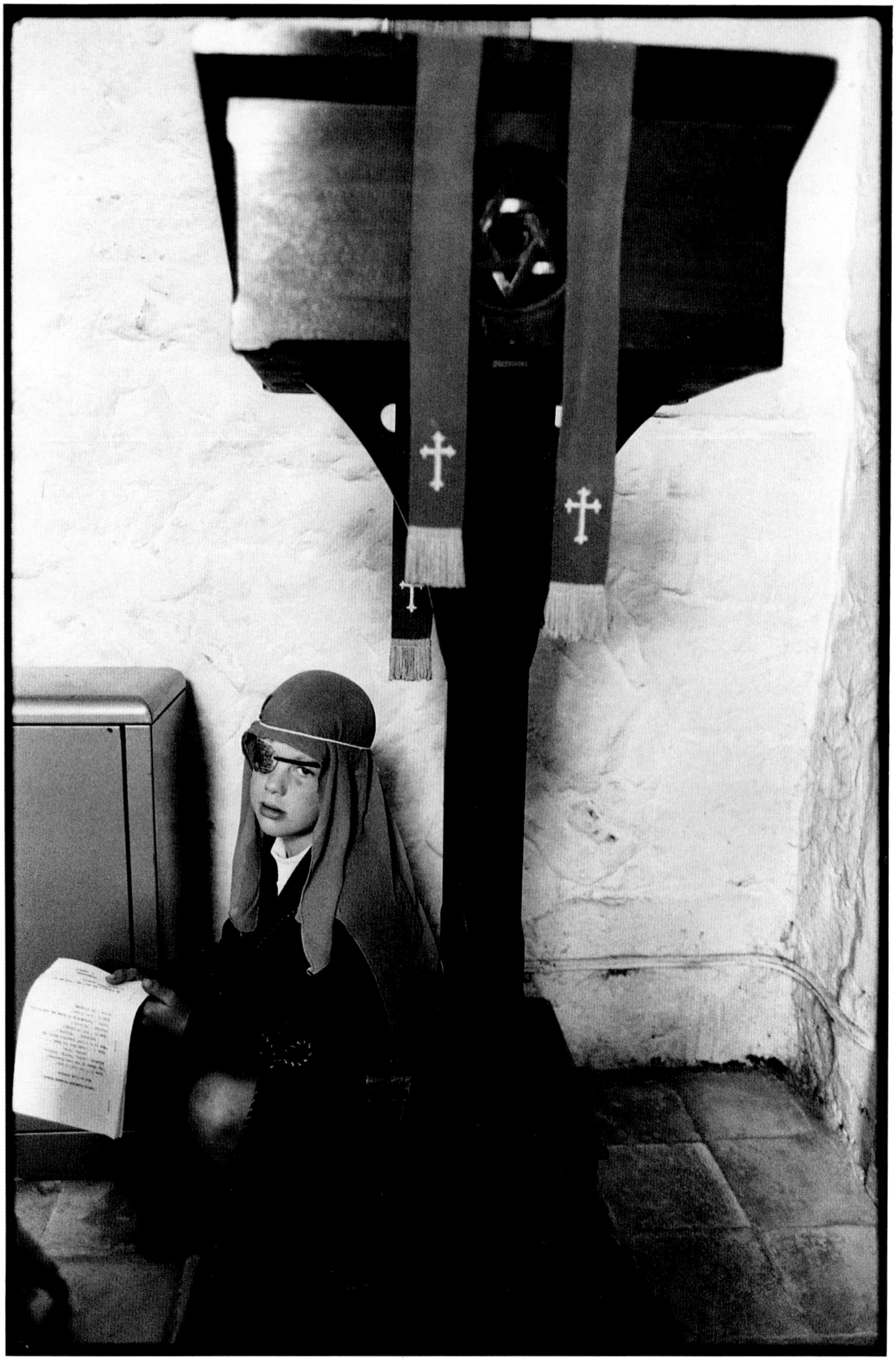

85

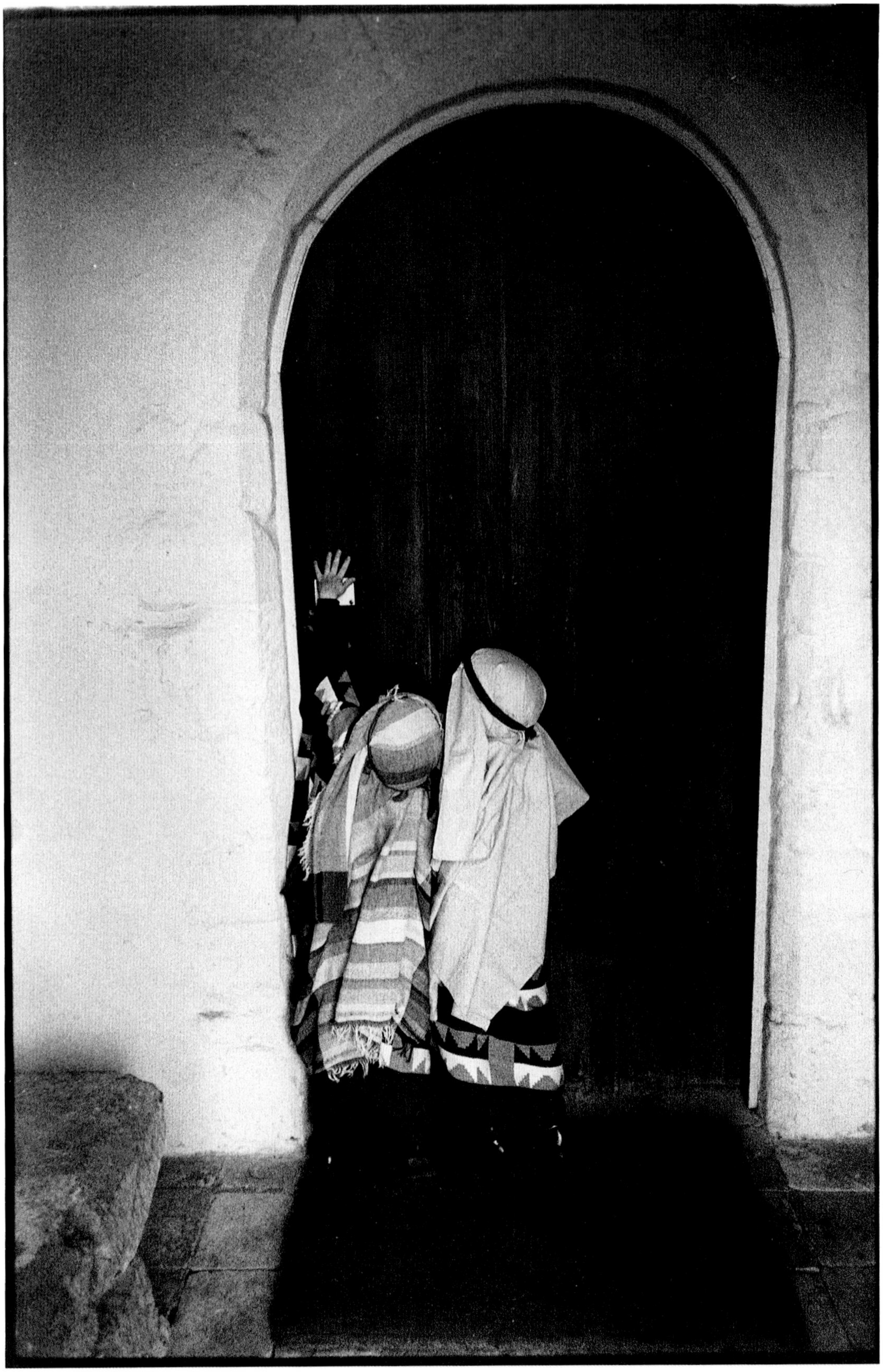

87

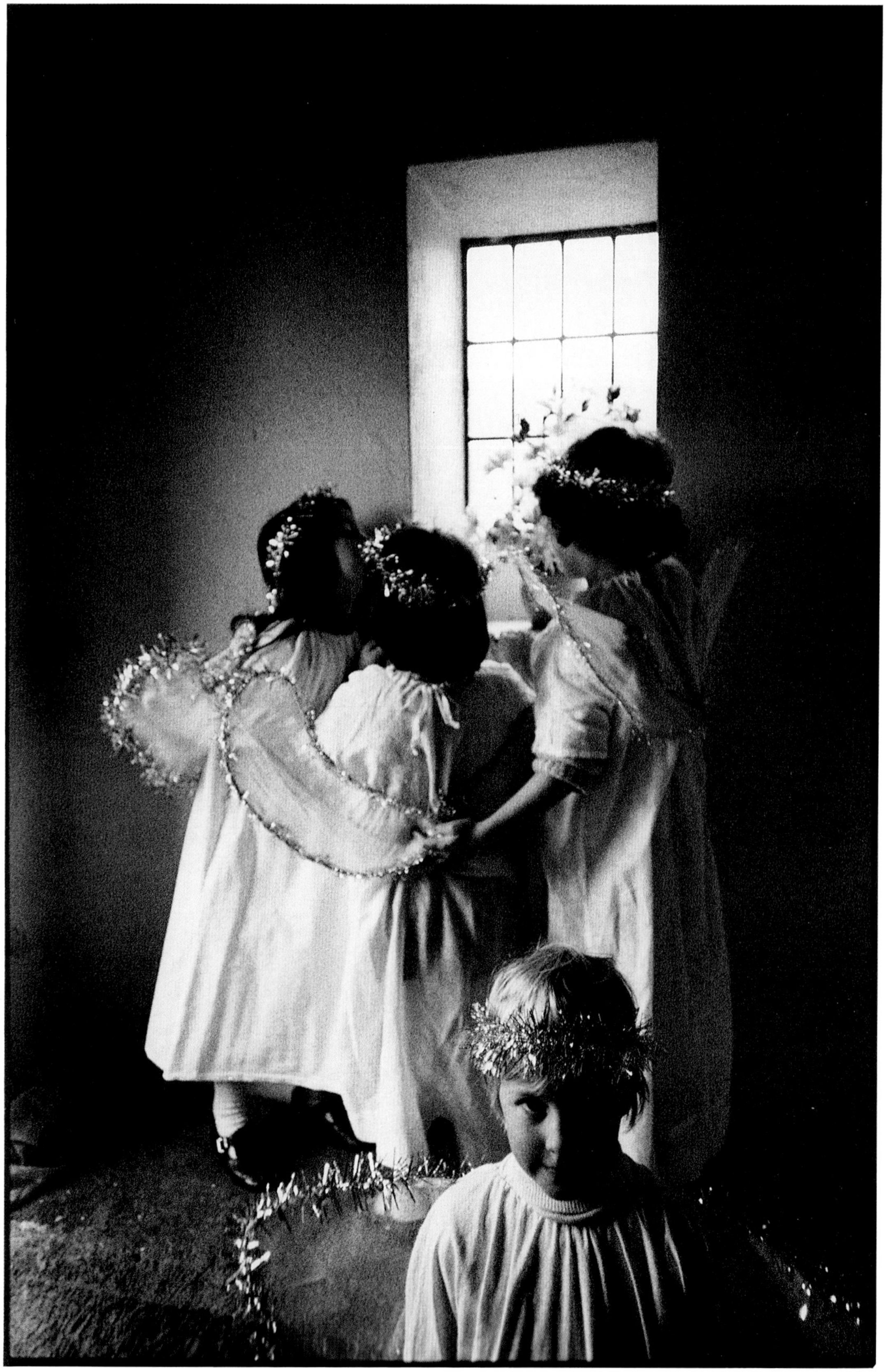

89

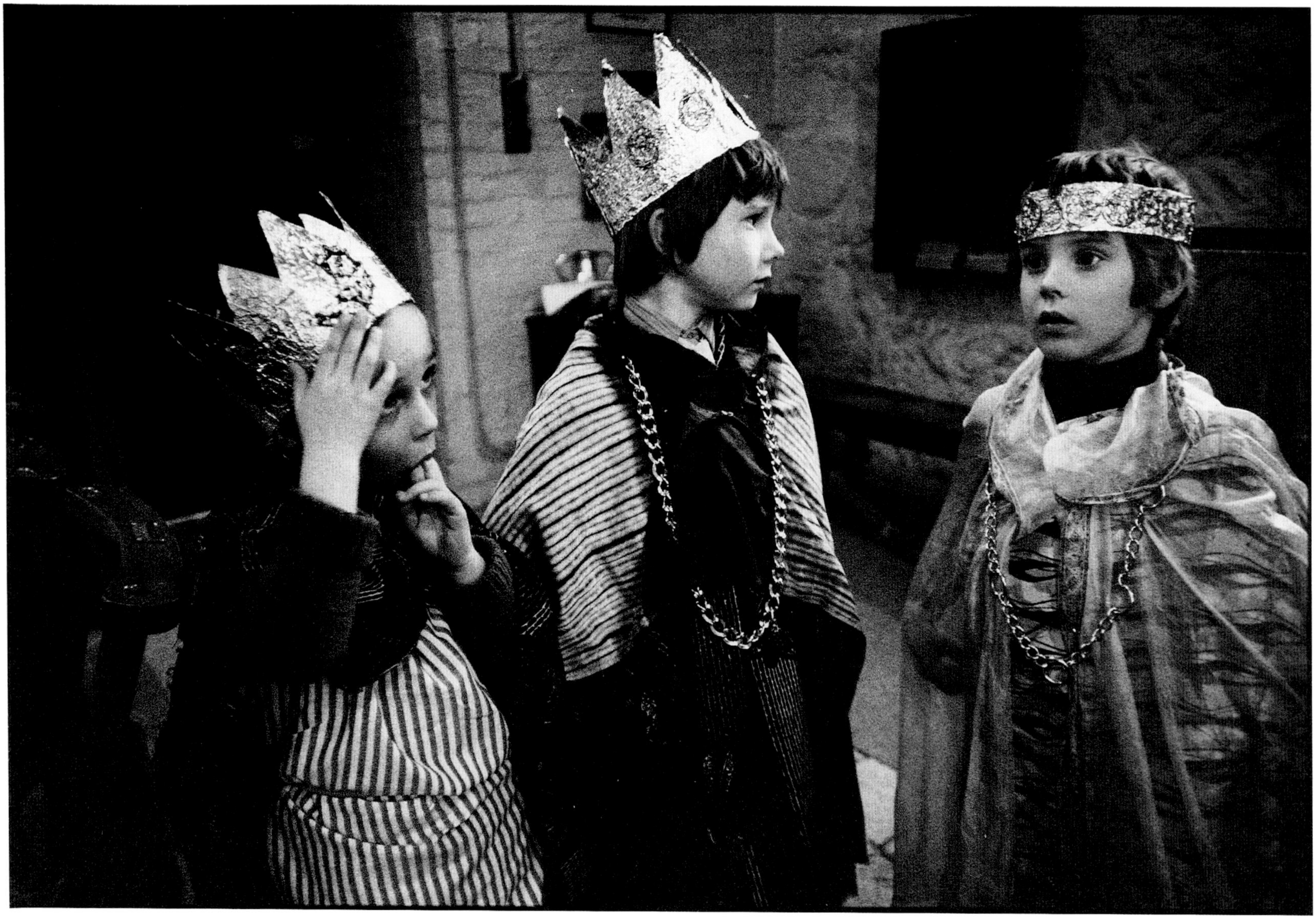

91

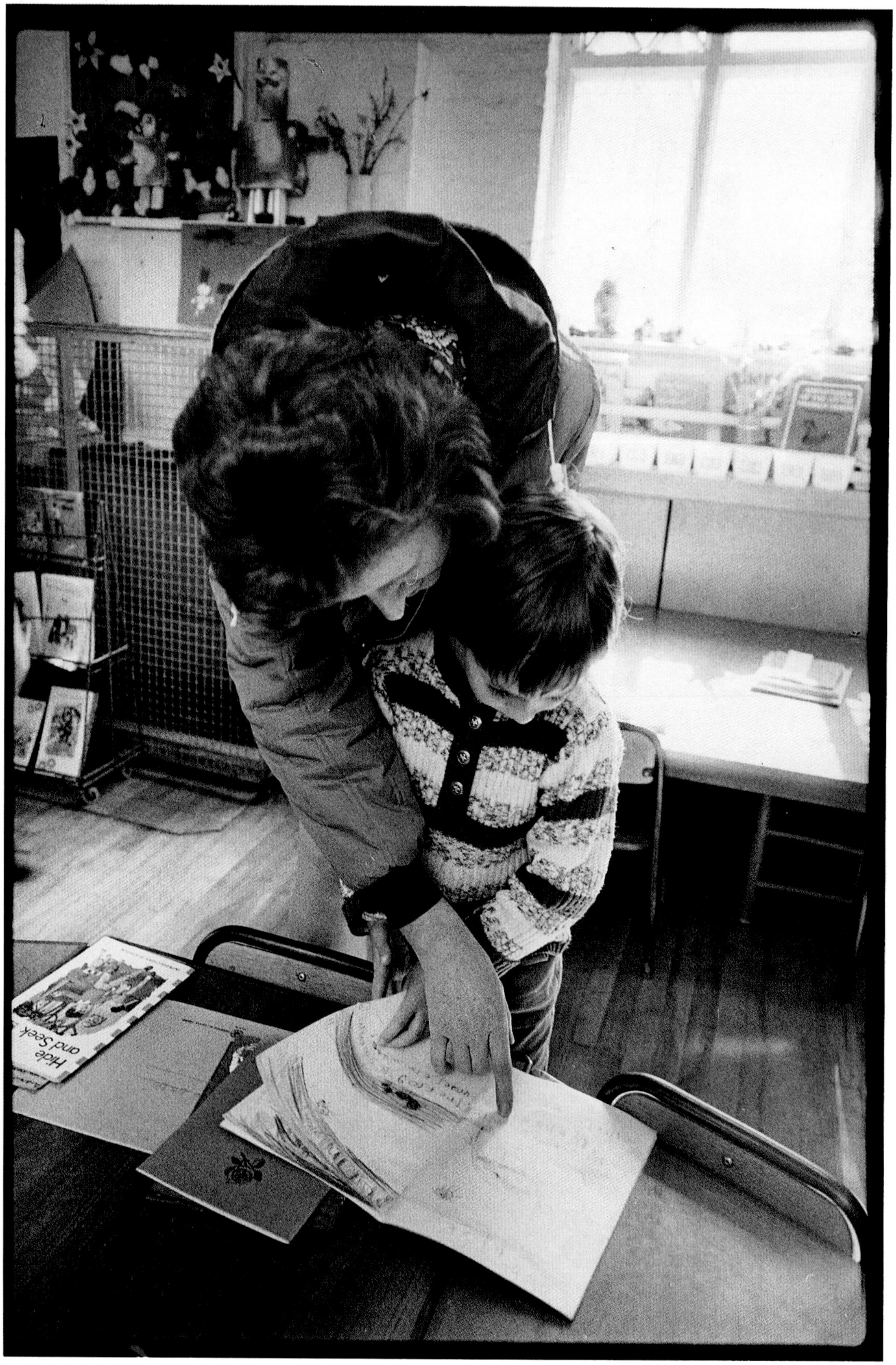
Hide
and Seek

93

94

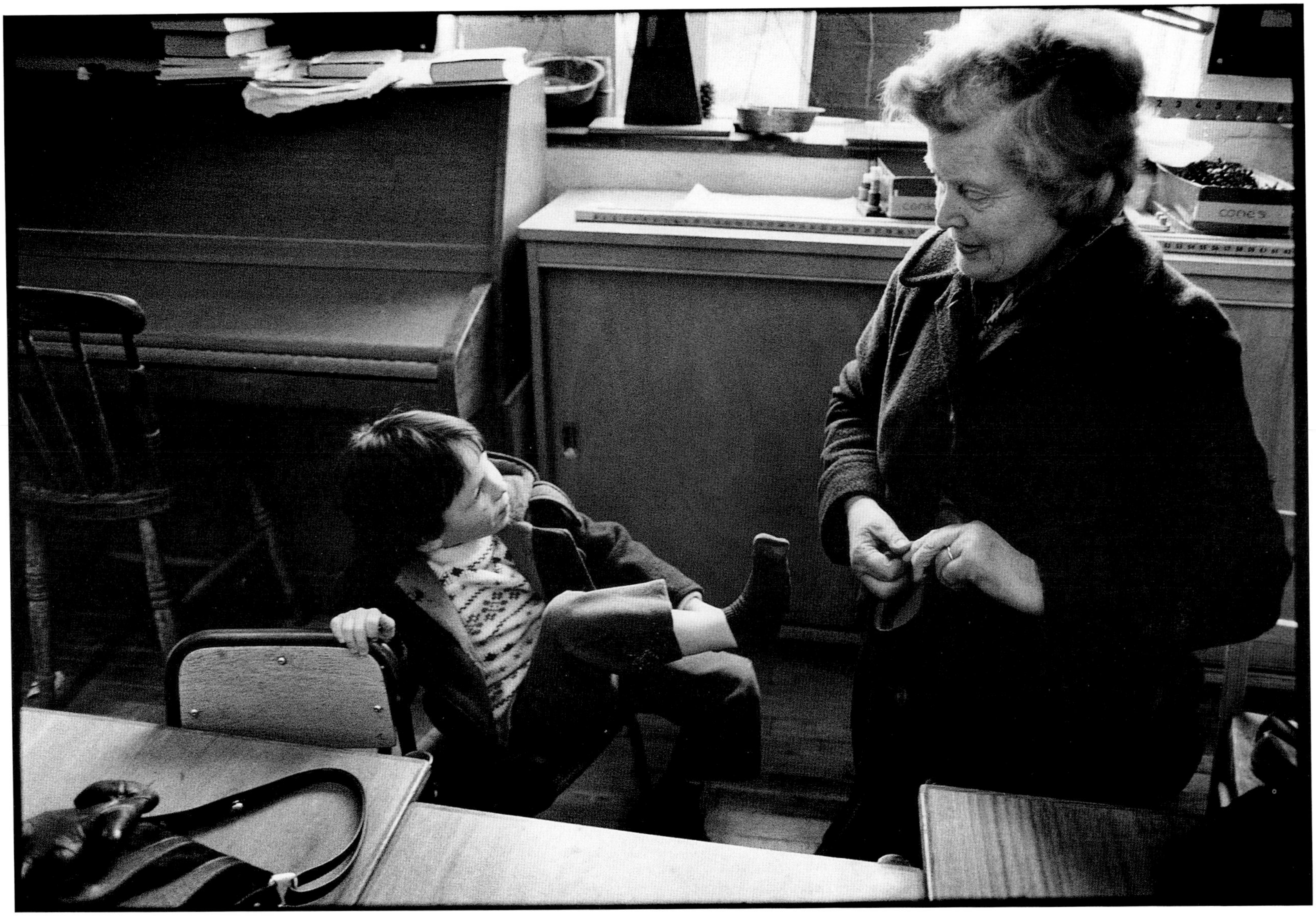

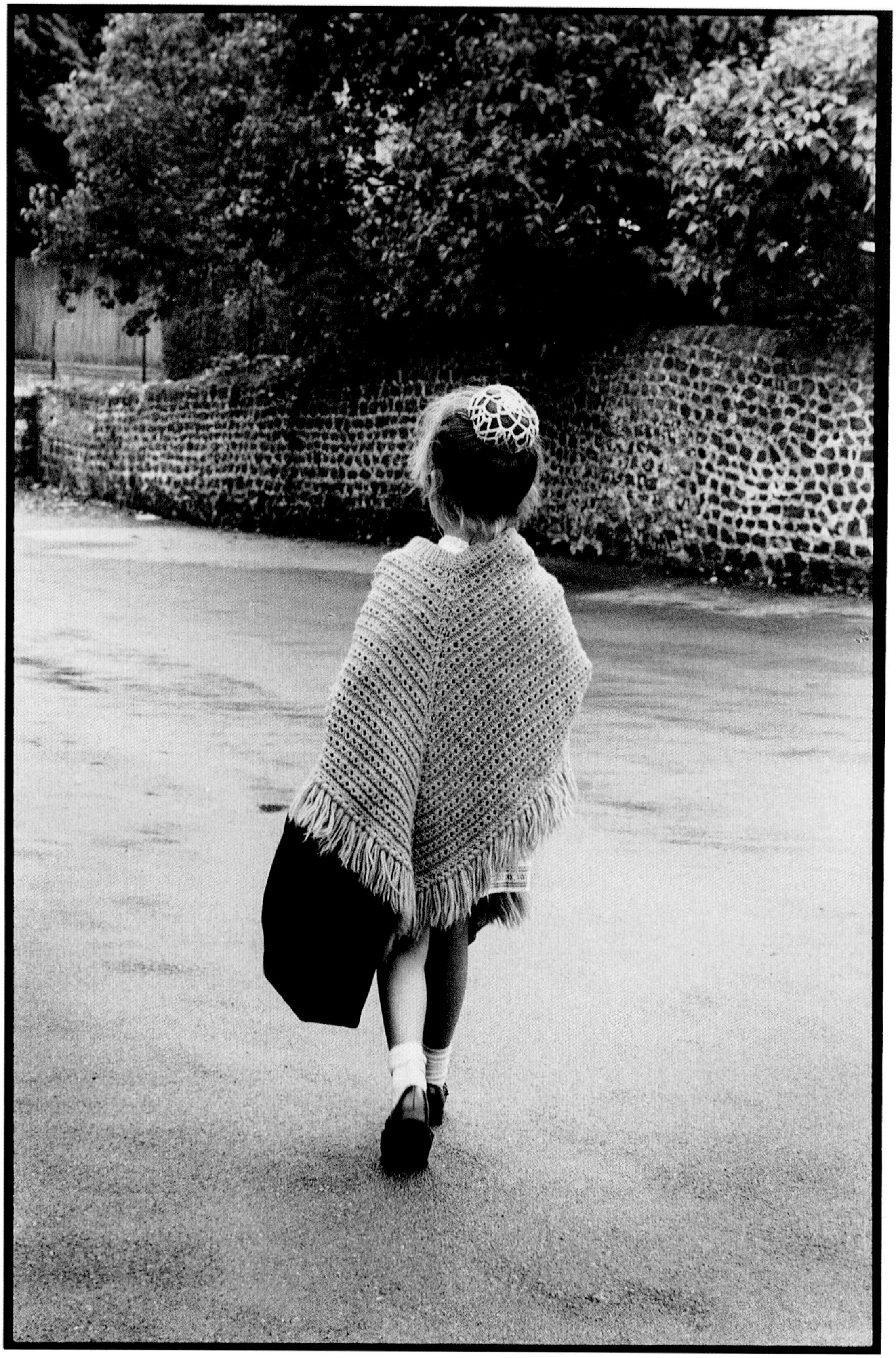

My thanks to : West Sussex County Council
for permission to carry out this project.

The Arts Council of Great Britain
for a grant in 1973 that covered the cost
of printing the photographs for exhibition.

Kodak Limited
for the award of a bursary in 1973 supporting
a further project, exhibited together with the
village school photographs under the title,
CARING & CONCERN, at the Kodak Photographic
Gallery in 1976.

Juan I-Jong and Nathalie Juan for their
encouragement and help in publishing this book.

CAPTIONS

1. Going to school.
2. A kiss for mother.
3. The school buildings.
4. Morning prayers.
5 - 33. In the classrooms.
8. Infants teacher, Miss Susan Bishop.
21. Headmistress, Mrs Audrey Campbell.
34. Nature study walk.
35. Outdoor art class.
36 - 40. Visit to a local farm.
40. Filmed by a TV crew.
41. Setting up lunch.
42 - 44. Lunchtime problems.
45 - 56. Playtime.
57. Casualty.
58 - 59. A game of draughts.
60. A visit from the retired infants teacher and regular helper, Miss Faith Head.
61. Pop group.
62. A parent, Mrs Manley, giving one of her weekly cookery lessons.
63 - 65. In the classrooms.
66 - 67. A talk by one of HM Coastguards.
68 - 71. Organised games.
72 - 79. The swimming pool was built and paid for by parents.
80 - 82. A visit to HMS Victory.
83. Harvest Festival preparations.
84 - 86. Dress rehearsal for staging the parable of The Good Samaritan at the village church.
87 - 90. Dress rehearsal for a Christmas Nativity play at the village church.
91 - 93. Parents examine their children's work.
94. Fund-raising sale.
95. A helping hand from the welfare assistant, Mrs E. Barnes.
96. Homeward bound.

BRYN CAMPBELL   BRIEF CHRONOLOGY

1933	Born in South Wales.
1951-58	National Service, RAF photographer - university - worked as industrial photographer - joined a Fleet Street picture agency - freelanced briefly.
1959-60	Assistant editor PRACTICAL PHOTOGRAPHY and PHOTO NEWS WEEKLY.
1960-61	Editor CAMERAS magazine.
1962-63	Associate Editor THE BRITISH JOURNAL OF PHOTOGRAPHY.
1963-64	Helped launch THE OBSERVER COLOUR MAGAZINE.
1964-66	Picture editor THE OBSERVER.
1966-72	Freelance photographer retained by THE OBSERVER.
1969	1st Prize (News) in British Press Pictures of the Year contest. Awarded fellowship of the BIPP.
1971	Awarded fellowship of the RPS. Official photographer of the British Headless Valley Expedition.
1972-73	Village School project.
1972-84	Freelance photographer/writer.
1973	Awarded Kodak Bursary.
1974-77	Awarded honorary associate lectureship in photographic arts by The Polytechnic of Central London.
1974-80	Acted as external examiner in photography to eight art colleges and polytechnics throughout the UK.
1974-84	Trustee of The Photographers' Gallery, London.
1975	Photographed end of the war in Vietnam.
1977-78	Member of the CNAA Photography Board.
1978	Wrote and presented six-part BBC TV series EXPLORING PHOTOGRAPHY.
1978-80	Member of Photography Committee, Arts Council of Great Britain.
1979-82	Official photographer of the Transglobe Expedition.
1980-83	Member of the Arts Panel, Arts Council of GB.
1984-85	Picture editor SUNDAY EXPRESS MAGAZINE.
1984-88	Chairman, Sports Pictures of the Year judging panel.
1985	British judge, WORLD PRESS PHOTO contest.
1985-87	Picture editor THE ILLUSTRATED LONDON NEWS.
1987-88	Picture editor DAILY TELEGRAPH MAGAZINE.
1988-93	Picture editor THE ILLUSTRATED LONDON NEWS.
1993 on	Freelance photographer and writer.

BOOKS

1963	THE BRITISH JOURNAL OF PHOTOGRAPHY ANNUAL. Picture editor.
1964	THE BRITISH JOURNAL OF PHOTOGRAPHY ANNUAL. Picture editor/designer.
1973	LONELINESS. Photographs. Text by Jeremy Seabrook.
1975	THE EXPERIENCE OF SPORT. Photographs. Various texts.
1976	CHILDREN AND LANGUAGE. Photographs. Various texts.
1976	THE FACTS ABOUT A FOOTBALL CLUB. Photographs. Text by Alan Road.
1977	NEWSPAPER DRAGON. Photographs. Text by Alan Road.
1977	GOALKEEPERS ARE CRAZY. Photographs. Text by Brian Glanville.
1978	EXPLORING PHOTOGRAPHY. Editor/writer. Accompanied BBC TV series.
1981	WORLD PHOTOGRAPHY. Editor/writer.
1982	I GRANDI FOTOGRAFI. Co-editor/writer. Italian series of 72 monographs on great photographers.
1983	THE GREAT PHOTOGRAPHERS. Consultant editor/writer. English editions of ten Italian monographs.
1983	GREAT ACTION PHOTOGRAPHY. Editor/writer.
1995	VILLAGE SCHOOL. Photographic project.
1995	THE IMPRECISE IMAGE. Experiments in colour photography.

MAJOR ONE-MAN EXHIBITIONS

1973	Retrospective. The Photographers' Gallery, London.
1975	Village School. Chichester 900 Festival.
1976	Caring and Concern. Kodak Gallery, London.
1978	Retrospective. Salzburg College, Austria.
1979	Experimental colour work. Salzburg College, Austria.
1980	Antarctic expedition. Olympus Gallery, London.
1981	Colour retrospective. The Photographers' Gallery, London.

First published in 1995 by Comus Books

All rights reserved. No part of this publication may be
reproduced or transmitted in any form or by any means,
electronic or mechanical, including photocopying,
recording or any information storage or retrieval system,
without written permission from the copyright owner.

© 1995 All photographs and text, copyright Bryn Campbell.

ISBN 0 - 9525197 - 0 - 4
British Library Cataloguing in Publication Data.
A catalogue record for this book is available from
the British Library.

Printed in Taiwan by SHEN's Art Printing Co., Ltd.